British Horror Films You Must Watch Before You Get Axed to Death

Thomas Baxter

CONTENTS

INTRODUCTION

The list of films that follows is by no means comprehensive or a list of the 'best' British horror films but it is a nice, slightly random collection of British horror films that everyone should get around to watching sooner or later. Some of the films that follow will be familiar (I'd imagine there are few people left in the world who haven't seen Shaun of the Dead or Don't Look Now) but there are, I hope, plenty of obscure ones too or films that, for one reason or another, you haven't got around to watching yet.

The golden age of British horror films was the salad days of Hammer - and Amicus had a pretty good run there too with their enjoyable anthology films. There was plenty of other good stuff out there though - like the Pete Walker films, Dr Phibes, Death Line, and so on. There have been a slew of new British horror films in more recent decades and an awful lot of them have been absolutely terrible. It's not all doom and gloom though because there have been some bright spots like The Descent, Censor, and Ghost Stories - all of which we'll cover in the book.

In this book I have also dipped into television because, for my money, some of the most terrifying British horror films ever made have come from that medium. I'm talking about things like Ghostwatch, Threads, and Whistle and I'll Come to You. When it comes to pure horror how can you top Threads? It is one of the most frightening things ever made - and all the more sobering because it depicts something which could ACTUALLY happen.

I've tried not to include too many films of a similar ilk or origin in this book. So, for example, as much as I love every one of the Amicus anthology films I have not included them all. In the same vein, I have not included all of the Hammer vampire films in the book because it would be a trifle samey if I did that. Not to say this book is devoid of Hammer vampire capers though because I'll have plenty to say about films like Dracula A.D 1972, The Legend of the 7 Golden Vampires and Twins of Evil.

So, strap yourselves in, make sure the doors are locked, blow out the candles, and prepare to enter the world of British horror films. A world of rural folk horror, megalithic stones, vampires, werewolves, escaped lunatics, nuclear war, Cenobites, zombies, spooky children, serial killers, cannibals, stone tapes, ghosts, elementals, killer cults, droogs, time loops, misty moors, nutty ventriloquists, graverobbers, rare and unusual objects of the occult, alien spaceships in the London Underground, Shakespeare inspired murders, and an archly eyebrowed Vanessa Howard.

THE ABOMINABLE DR PHIBES (1971)

The Abominable Dr Phibes was directed by Robert Fuest and written by William Goldstein and James Whiton. Dr Anton Phibes (Vincent Price) is a brilliant scholar and organist who was presumed dead in a 1921 car crash after hearing of the death of his wife Victoria (played by Hammer star Caroline Munro) during surgery. It turns out that Phibes is not dead. He's very much alive - although badly injured and he now wears a prosthetic mask and can only speak through an electrical voice device. Phibes seeks revenge against the doctors he blames for not saving his beloved wife and plans to kill them using the ten plagues of Egypt as his inspiration...

The Abominable Dr Phibes is one of the best cult horror films of the seventies and a fantastically bizarre and stylish experience. Very rarely will you see a modestly budgeted horror film look so fantastic. The art deco designs of Phibes' lair are a lot fun. Phibes has a beautiful mute assistant named Vulnavia (played by Virginia North) who he likes to dance with and a musical band of automata. He is truly one of the most unique and enjoyable horror villains imaginable. Phibes is like a horror supervillain with his theatrics and grand lair. The manner in which he can temporarily repair his face rather anticipates Sam Raimi's Darkman.

The deaths are naturally the main fun of the film and enjoyably inventive. The 'death by frog mask' scene has some striking imagery and I especially like the death by locusts scene too, amusingly improbable as it is. Price makes a great mute villain and proves what a fine charismatic actor he was. One could easily imagine Price making a fine silent film actor even without that wonderful voice. The Phibes films seem to be the template for the similar (if nastier) Theatre of Blood film that Price made in 1973. All these films feature Price as an eccentric, theatrical and unfathomable avenger out on a macabre mission of elaborate skewed justice. They also give the Price character a beautiful female assistant (in the case of

Theatre of Blood it was obviously Diana Rigg as Lionheart's loyal daughter).

Joseph Cotten is the main actor away from Price as Dr Vesalius and helps the film by playing it fairly straight in the midst of all the camp. Dr Vesalius was supposed to be played by Peter Cushing but, sadly, he had to withdraw when his wife fell ill. The Abominable Dr Phibes would have been even more cultish with Price AND Cushing. Peter Jeffrey plays Inspector Harry Trout on the trail of Phibes and there's a terrific supporting turn by Terry Thomas. His character has all of his blood removed by Dr Phibes and placed in jars! The big showdown scene is interesting as it presents Vesalius with a medical task which involves his son in great danger. The trap that his son is in almost seems to anticipate more modern horror films like the Saw franchise and the Cube movies.

For my money, the funniest supporting performance in the film comes from Aubrey Woods as a jeweller who Inspector Trout visits to learn more about an amulet found at one of the crime scenes. Look out by the way for Dad's Army star John Laurie too. The direction in the film is incredibly inventive and superbly orchestrated, giving scenes a strange dreamlike feel. The music score is very 1920s and only adds to the bizarre aura that hovers over The Abominable Dr Phibes. This is a really fun film with plenty of familiar faces, incredible art direction and sets, lots of striking imagery, amusing death scenes, and a spellbinding performance by Price as the mournful Phibes.

Though he does some awful things, Phibes is a more sympathetic character than Edward Lionheart in Theatre of Blood because he is motivated by his broken heart. You actually feel a bit sorry for him at times. Although to be fair, Lionheart probably does have a slightly better motive in that he is murdering a bunch of snooty critics who mocked his acting. It seems a trifle unfair for Phibes to target these doctors because it isn't as if they let Victoria die on purpose! The Abominable Dr Phibes is one of the best cult British horrors of the seventies and makes a great double bill with its sequel - which we shall of course later get around to in this book.

THE ABOMINABLE SNOWMAN (1957)

The Abominable Snowman is an early and slightly overlooked 1957 horror film from the legendary Hammer Studios, directed by Val Guest and written by the always interesting Nigel Kneale - who adapted the screenplay from his own BBC teleplay called The Creature. The film is set high in the Himalayas where British botanist and ex-mountain climber Dr John Rollason (the great Peter Cushing) is working and occasionally musing on the existence of the Yeti - the mysterious ape-like creature that some believe lurks somewhere in the frozen wastes of the mountains.

The arrival of a plucky team of American explorers led by the somewhat dodgy and opportunist Dr Tom Friend (Forrest Tucker) manages to pique Rollason's interest and scientific curiosity when it becomes apparent that they intend to launch a daring search for proof of this legendary beast. Despite protests from his nervous wife Helen (Maureen Connell) and mysterious warnings from the enigmatic Llama (Arnold Marle) of the local Tibetan monastery, Rollason agrees to join the Americans on their expedition climb.

But as they painstakingly make their way up the icy and treacherous surroundings in search of the mythical Yeti, they begin to encounter distinct attempts to sabotage the expedition and that's the very least of problems. Of more pressing concern is a raid on their camp by a mysterious creature and increasingly weird and troubling events that begin to slowly unhinge the members of the search team...

An interesting early offering from Hammer that seems to have got a bit lost over the years in amongst the studio's more famous and usual colour gothic fare, The Abominable Snowman is a decent and interesting attempt to make an intelligent monster film with vague sci-fi elements and is always pleasantly atmospheric with the wild, bleak setting, black and white photography and eerie sound-effects of strange howls away in the distance and severe winds battering the snow-capped mountain. The film is mildly intriguing right from the start with the mysterious Llama character and his cryptic warnings to Cushing's Rollason and the well-designed monastery sets and inventive studio snowscapes are really good at times.

There's a nice contrast too between the urbane and very English Peter Cushing and the louder and somewhat more boisterous Forrest Tucker as the head of the American Yeti expedition. Peter Cushing was of course wonderful in absolutely anything he did and is as watchable as ever as the restrained and intelligent Rollason - who he makes warm and very likeable in his usual polished, gentle and winning fashion. The very American Forest Tucker, presumably cast to give the film more international appeal, is fine too and, although vaguely the baddie here, does make his character more or less decent at heart.

Look too for Robert Brown as the expert animal tracker Ed Shelley. Brown later played M in the two Timothy Dalton James Bond films. The Abominable Snowman becomes gradually more thoughtful and weirder as it progresses with various attempts by locals to stop the expedition for reasons that are never quite made clear. It perhaps betrays its television roots by being rather talky at times but the picture is always absorbing and the dialogue and ideas prevent The Abominable Snowman from ever sinking into kitsch throwaway fifties monster picture mode too much.

Kneale includes a subtext about the dangers of meddling with things we don't fully understand and comes up with a decent and memorable ending too which leaves some food for thought. Nigel Kneale's work tends to have a pessimistic note with humankind always on the cusp of possible extinction by forces greater than ourselves and ripe for the taking and the creatures atop the mountain have slightly ambiguous origins and designs which adds a layer of interest to the story and makes the viewer think for themselves.

The intentions of the Llama are also slightly vague too which I quite liked. We are never quite sure if he is completely manipulating Rollason and if he is for what distinct purpose. The expedition team set animal traps in an attempt to catch a Yeti much to the dismay of Rollason ("Of all the idiotic, maniac ideas!") who gradually suspects that the creatures might have spooky telepathic powers and may be slowly driving the expedition members insane on purpose. "This creature may have an affinity for man, something in common with ourselves. Let's remember that before we start shooting," he warns, urging a note of caution.

The studio sets used in The Abominable Snowman are quite effective onscreen and mesh relatively well with the location footage shot in the Pyrenees for the film - this footage adding a real bit of scope to proceedings. Although not a big film, The Abominable Snowman is admirably inventive and creative with its relatively modest budget. The shots of the expedition climbing are nicely done too although somewhat limited and sparingly deployed and the competent Val Guest gives the film a tight, taut, atmospheric feel to hide the constrictive budget, this always working well enough on the whole I think.

The Abominable Snowman is certainly eerie and mildly creepy and has one or two slightly cheesy shocks such as when a rather hairy arm reaches inside a tent to great alarm as you'd expect. Dr Rollason soon begins to have problems with the methods and aims of the expedition and realises Friend is a bit of a publicity seeker. "You're nothing but a cheap fairground trickster!" One other plus for the film is the orchestral soundtrack which adds a touch of sweep to the climbing sequences. This is certainly, in my opinion, a fun film to watch late at night with all the lights off so you can become fully immersed in the windswept, icy atmosphere with the vaguely supernatural and spooky touches.

The Abominable Snowman is decent fun on the whole and perhaps stands as one of the more forgotten and underrated Hammer entries. Any film with Peter Cushing is worth a look and this is certainly no exception with a good, taut atmosphere and one or two creepy and thought provoking moments courtesy of the script by Nigel Kneale, a writer who understood how important building tension and atmosphere is to these types of stories.

AN AMERICAN WEREWOLF IN LONDON (1981)

Is it pushing things to call An American Werewolf in London a British film - given that it was made by an American studio? I suppose we can half claim it because it was a British co-production and obviously has a very British sensibility given that it is set in Blighty and has a British supporting cast. An American Werewolf in London was written and directed by John Landis.

Landis was pretty hot stuff around this time and had recently directed Animal House and The Blues Brothers. His career was tarnished by the Twilight Zone tragedy though and he never really fufilled his early promise. An American Werewolf in London is a very interesting film because it is plainly made by someone who loves horror films and knows how to scare you but also by someone with a sense of humour who knows how to get a laugh. It is very difficult to get the balance between humour and horror right in a film like this but An American Werewolf in London manages to pull off that tricky task.

Does anyone not know the plot of An American Werewolf in London by now? Two American backpackers - David (David

Naughton) and Jack (Griffin Dunne) - are attacked on the Yorkshire moors by a large creature. Jack is killed and David wakes up in hospital in London - where he takes a shine to Jenny Agutter's nurse. It transpires that they were attacked by a werewolf. As he was bitten, David should probably be wary of the next full moon...

1981 was the year of the werewolf film. We had Joe Dante's The Howling, the mystical Wolfen, and An American Werewolf in London. An American Werewolf in London is the best of that trio. This is justifiably considered to be one of the greatest werewolf films ever made. The secret to its success is that although it could be described as a horror comedy , as the offbeat wit of John Landis is very much present, it is also genuinely frightening too with some incredible 'jump' scares and plenty of blood. The opening werewolf attack on the moors is absolutely terrifying. I gather that John Landis wanted to make this scene as harrowing as possible to let the audience know that while An American Werewolf in London had a sense of humour it would also be a full blooded horror film.

There are so many memorable scenes in the film - right from the start when David and Jack enter a very isolated pub full of strange locals who warn them to stay off the moors and stick to the roads. Not the friendliest pub in the world I must say! The interior of The Slaughtered Lamb was filmed back in London and the pub's clientele consists mostly of local stage actors. Rik Mayall was invited to be in the film (Mayall is one of the characters in the Slaughtered Lamb) after John Landis saw him perform at a comedy club.

Thc device whereby David learns that he is a werewolf is a clever and interesting one. It comes to him in the form of the dead Jack. Jack is resigned to a 'living death' in limbo unless the werewolf line is broken by David killing himself. Naturally, David isn't too convinced at first by the claims of his ghostly friend that he needs to commit suicide. Jack seems to decompose more and more through the film whenever he appears to David and Landis makes him look increasingly gross with some relish.

Naughton and Griffin Dunne have some genuine comic chemistry and play off one another well in their scenes together. The juxtaposition of the deadpan banter between the pair and Griffin Dunne's increasingly gruesome visage is black humour at its finest. Universal had wanted Dan Aykroyd and John Belushi to play the leads but Landis didn't like this idea because he thought people would then expect a spoof or full blown comedy. David Naughton (who was best known for Dr Pepper commercials) and Griffin Dunne turn out to be inspired casting.

One can't talk about this film either without mentioning the incredible werewolf transformation scene by Rick Baker - a true masterclass that beats anything you'll see in today's CGI age. The remarkable thing about this sequence is that it is done in full light and yet we believe in it completely. David's transformation scene took six days to shoot. The nightmare sequences in the film too are deservedly revered and terrifying. Landis gets one of the best 'jump' scares in horror history in these sequences.

Another great thing about the film is the way that Landis uses the setting to gently mock (in an affectionate way) but also celebrate British understatement. The dry humour of Landis meshes well with the very English sensibility of the supporting characters. Trivia - because David calls Prince Charles' sexuality into question in the film, a disclaimer was added to the credits which read "Lycanthrope films limited wishes to extend its heartfelt congratulations to Lady Diana Spencer and His Royal Highness the Prince of Wales on the occasion of their marriage - July 29th 1981".

This is also one of those films which taps into the strangeness of the London Underground and exploits that for horror purposes. The London Underground station used in the film is Tottenham Court Road. When David transforms into a werewolf he prowls the tube looking for victims and Landis throws his camera around the little tunnels with great panache. The escalator shot where we glimpse the werewolf is very striking. The film has some dramatic heart too, like the moment where David phones his family to say goodbye and the romance that develops between him and Jenny Agutter's nurse. An American Werewolf in London is a truly unique experience in the way that it fuses together a comedic sensibility with a full throttle horror film. It remains good scary fun.

AND SOON THE DARKNESS (1970)

And Soon the Darkness was directed by Robert Fuest (who would go on to direct Vincent Price in the Dr Phibes films) and written by Brian Clemens and Terry Nation. Two young nurses from England named Jane (Pamela Franklin) and Cathy (Michele Dotrice) are on a cycling holiday in a rural part of France. The two women begin to bicker and argue though when they disagree on the itinery and Jane cycles off in a huff - leaving Cathy to sunbathe alone in some woods with her radio.

Jane decides to go back for Cathy in the end but Cathy is gone. It seems that someone was stalking Cathy in the woods. Jane cycles around searching for clues about where Cathy might be but only draws a frustrating blank. The fact that she can't speak French is obviously not a tremendous help either. Alarmingly, Jane hears that the local area is considered dangerous and there was a recent murder of a woman. A young man named Paul (Sandor Elès), who claims to be a former policc officer and was spotted earlier by Cathy at a roadside cafe, decides to help Jane but can he be trusted? And what on earth happened to Cathy anyway? With her trusty bicycle and a steady supply of soft fruit drinks, Jane attempts to solve this mystery...

And Soon the Darkness, rather strangely, seems to have little to no reputation at all when it comes to British thriller/horror films. Many critics at the time seemed to find this to be a mediocre film in which not a lot happens - and slowly at that. I can't say I personally agree with that consensus at all. And Soon the Darkness is a rare and interesting example of a daylight horror film and the little stretch of flat French countryside (the film was shot on location in France too) becomes weird and eerie in a subtle sort of way. Compared to modern horror thrillers, And Soon the Darkness is a model of restraint and this keeps the film on an even keel and makes it feel more plausible. If this film was made today they'd have endless murders in the film and Jane would probably end up being chased by some maniac in a truck or something just so they could have an action sequence. And Soon the Darkness is more about mood and mystery than shocks. The main shocks are saved for the end in And Soon the Darkness.

You wouldn't think that a young woman cycling up and down a stretch of road would be the best ingredient for a thriller film but And Soon the Darkness is quietly compelling and does make you genuinely interested to see how it all pans out. The film rests squarely on the shoulders of Pamela Franklin as Jane is the main character for nearly all of the running time and our window into the story. Franklin, with bob haircut, a natty blue neckscarf and shorts, is an appealing and human heroine who ends up in this puzzling situation where she is trying to find out where her friend is but isn't sure who she can trust. Jane is a bit out of her depth but compensates for this with her determination and dogged refusal to give up. There are a number of red herrings thrown in our direction over the course of the film before all is revealed at the end.

Pamela Franklin was a talented child and teen actor but she got rather typecast in the end by appearing in a few too many horror films. In her last film, Franklin suffered the indignity of appearing in Bert I. Gordon's preposterous 1976 low-budget nonsense The Food of the Gods (the film with giant rats if you please). Franklin only had a few television roles after that and retired to concentrate on family life. It's a shame really because she seemed destined for bigger things. Michele Dotrice, or Mrs Frank Spencer as she's more commonly known, isn't in the film for very long but makes her mark.

Sandor Elès is appropriately ambiguous as the suave Paul. Is he really trying to help or is he up to something? John Nettleton, who plays the Gendarme at the police station who Jane goes to for help, is a very familiar face. You've seen him in everything from Yes, Minister to Minder to Midsomer Murders. There aren't actually that many actors in And Soon the Darkness - which helps to convey the increasing sense of isolation felt by Jane in the story. One clever device is that Jane can't speak French and when other characters are speaking French to her we don't get any subtitles. This means that (unless one can speak French) we are as much in the dark as Jane and so feel her sense of confusion.

And Soon the Darkness is an interesting suspense thriller with moments of horror. Pamela Franklin does most of the heavy lifting in what is a fairly solo sort of spotlight but she's well up to the task. This film is definitely worth watching if you've never seen it before. It probably won't be everyone's cup of tea due to the sedate pacing but as long as you aren't expecting a high body count and loads of gore the film is very rewarding. You won't be surprised to hear that, many years later, And Soon the Darkness got a positively awful American remake. Give that one a very wide bearth and stick with the original.

THE APPOINTMENT (1982)

The Appointment was directed Lindsey C. Vickers - who worked on some of the Hammer films and had previously directed a short film called The Lake. The frustrating treatment of The Appointment meant he never directed anything again - which is a shame. The Appointment was financed by the National Coal Board Pension Fund and was proposed as one of a number of television films which would make up a sort of anthology series. The other films did not transpire though and The Appointment did not get a cinema release. It was available on video for a time but then became a lost film that had been completely forgotten. Thankfully it was recently rediscovered and given a DVD release.

The film takes place in the Home Counties. It begins with a schoolgirl named Sandy (Auriol Goldingham) walking along a footpath by the woods after school. She's part of the school orchestra and carries a violin case. Voices call out to her from the woods and she's violently dragged away by an unseen force. Holy cripes. This scene is terrifying. What an opening! These early scenes have a voiceover of a police officer reading the reports on Sandy's disappearance. They soon drop the voiceover though.

You think that the film is going to be about the mystery of what happened to Sandy but it isn't at all. The film then changes into a strange and sometimes unfathomable psychological drama. The Appointment is always weirdly compelling though and plays a bit like a very bizarre episode of Hammer House of Mystery & Suspense. What is the main plot of The Appointment? Ian (the great Edward Woodward in a very large pair of glasses) lives in a nice house with his wife Dianna (Jane Merrow) and 14 year-old daughter Joanne (Samantha Weysom). Joanne seems to have a very close bond with her father and is devastated when she learns he can't attend her school music concert (she's a talented violinist) because he has to attend some sort of work related meeting many miles away.

Joanne throws a giant strop and although Ian feels guilty he decides he has no choice because the work related meeting is very important. That night Ian dreams about his car being attacked by rottweilers. His wife also has strange dreams. On his long drive to his meeting, Ian seems to keep encountering a lorry with rottweilers on the side. Meanwhile, we see Joanne talking to something unseen by the (now fenced off) woods where Sandy vanished. What can any of this mean?

The Appointment is not one of those films that gives you all the answers so you have to fill in some of the blanks for yourself. It seems pretty obvious though that Joanne has some sort of psychic ability - or dark powers. There is an obvious link between Sandy and Joanne which may (or may not) be significant. The film also appears to suggest that there might be something unhealthy going on between Ian and his daughter in that she is very possessive of him. Ian goes to enter Joanne's room at night but then decides not to. It seems unlikely that this subtext was unwitting or unintentional. Samantha Weysom (who has no acting credits beyond 1991) gives a rather bizarre performance with an odd (and wooden) line delivery but you know what? It actually works for the character. It makes Joanne seem weird.

It is sometimes said that this film is not horror and has no gore but that's not true. It has a consistently unsettling atmosphere thanks to the sound effects and score and a mechanic meets a very nasty end at one point. The film jumbles up dreams and reality in an effective way so sometimes you aren't quite sure what is real. Much of the film is just Edward Woodward driving in his car and, blimey, what a journey. It seems as if he drives halfway around the world! I bet that was part of the appeal for Edward Woodwood in taking this film was that he'd get to sit down for most of it! Why not just take the train? He'd surely get to his destination quicker!

The car crash sequence near the end is utterly brilliant. It's sort of ridiculous at first but then becomes terrifying when the car flips up over a precarious drop. The sequence where Ian is all bloodied and dazed and trapped in his car (which is perched in trees!) is both gripping and frightening. There's some nice outdoor location work in the driving scenes. Woodward earns his money with this crash sequence alone. The Appointment is a fascinating thriller/horror that deserved a wider audience. It's a shame really that it didn't get more attention. It would have made a great episode in either of the 1980s Hammer television shows. This film might be a bit slow for some but it is worth sticking with and is one of those films that lingers in the memory for a while after you've seen it.

THE BEAST MUST DIE (1974)

The Beast Must Die is a somewhat camp (at the very least it teeters on the brink in unsteady fashion) 1974 British horror film from the wonderful Amicus studio directed by Paul Annett and based on James Blish's story There Shall Be No Darkness. In the film wealthy playboy, philanthropist and big game hunter Tom Newcliffe (Calvin Lockhart) invites, as you do, an eclectic group of people to his gigantic country mansion as guests of him and his wife Caroline (Marlene Clark) because he is convinced that one of these characters is a werewolf! The sprawling mansion is fitted with a high-tech closed-circuit television surveillance system with numerous security cameras and listening devices controlled by Newcliffe's trusted assistant and employee Pavel (Anton Diffring). Once the werewolf is secretly spied or duly reveals his or her self Newcliffe plans to shoot the biggest game of all with his hunting rifle and add it to his prized trophy collection.

This select group of suspects is made up of archaeology and werewolf expert Dr Lundgren (Peter Cushing), former medical student and suspected cannibal Paul Foote (Tom Chadbon), disgraced British diplomat with constantly disappearing staff Arthur Bennington (Charles Gray), society beauty Davinia Gilmore (Ciaran Madden), and shifty looking concert pianist Jan Jarmokowski (Michael Gambon), a man who (suspiciously) never seems too geographically far away from the scene of some grisly murder. "Why do you think I invited you? Because every one of you sitting right here in this room has one thing in common: Death!" declares Newcliffe. He's completely obsessed with bagging a werewolf and dismisses the servants and cuts off the telephones. He insists that his guests all stay throughout the cycle of the full moon until the beast reveals itself...

As our suspects play chess, banter, dine and discuss werewolf lore at Newcliffe's grand country house, numerous red herrings and clues are thrown in our direction and the film even invites us to guess who we think the werewolf might be, supplying us with an enjoyably gimmicky William Castle style thirty second 'Werewolf Break' (narrated by Valentine Dyall) with ticking clock before the great revelation. The Beast Must Die begins by telling us that "This is a detective story in which YOU are the detective. The question is not Who is the murderer? - But Who is the werewolf? After all the clues have been shown you will get a chance to give your answer. Watch for the werewolf break!"

The Beast Must Die is sort of Agatha Christie meets Shaft (leading man Calvin Lockhart comes across a more theatrical Shaft clone) meets The Most Dangerous Game meets James Bond meets a, er, daft low-budget Amicus film. It begins with some wonderfully funky and amusing seventies music courtesy of the always dependable Douglas Gamely and sweeping overhead shots of isolated countryside. Calvin Lockhart, wearing the first in a succession of slightly camp tight outfits that frequently make him look like a backing singer in the Eurovision song contest, is being hunted in a booby trapped forest by numerous armed men. He eventually crashes exhausted through the foliage onto genteel lawns by his mansion where his guests/werewolf suspects are politely sipping tea outside and waiting for him. The armed men of course were all Newcliffe employees and he was merely testing his security system using himself as bait.

The guests must know why they are really here and quickly start to bicker and look shifty when Newcliffe drops his - on the face of it completely bonkers - werewolf bombshell. "You're not seriously trying to tell us that one of us is a Werewolf!" protests Michael Gambon, looking a bit like Jason King. It's quite a nice idea to try and cross a drawing room murder mystery with a werewolf film and The Beast Must Die always keeps you reasonably interested to find out who the culprit is, especially when the murders begin. The clues and red herrings are a bit all over the place though to say the least and not to be taken too seriously. This is really a film where they could probably have revealed anyone as the werewolf at the end after endowing virtually every single character in the whole film with at least one suspicious piece of behaviour or background information!

The film makes quite good use of the surrounding woods (the famous Amicus stream makes an appearance), overhead helicopter shots and the whole surveillance angle. Pavel's security room with countless television monitors watching over the mansion is nicely designed and enjoyable in a dated seventies sort of way with its chessboard floor and Pavel's electronic "grid" with little red lights indicating where his various listening devices are. The scenes between Diffring and Lockhart in the security room as they plot a way to flush out the werewolf are always good fun. There is a car chase too involving Gambon that is slightly comical but enjoyable with Gamely's very seventies music pounding away. Perhaps one criticism is that the film is never very scary or frightening, instead often coming across as camp, but it is quite creepy on one or two occasions and there is a bit of blood and gore (though not much) here and there when the guests start to be picked off. One of the most atmospheric and memorable scenes in the film probably occurs when Pavel's security room is threatened by the werewolf from a glass ceiling high above.

The werewolf itself, when it finally makes an appearance, is quite obviously a large German Shepard dog with a big coat thrown over it or something and as you are always patently aware of this fact they wisely don't overdo the werewolf capers. At least you get a vague sense of a live beast on the loose even if it isn't terribly convincing or terrifying. The alternative of an actor pitching up with a Dog Soldiers type werewolf mask probably wouldn't have improved the film an awful lot in my opinion. The werewolf shenanigans work best when they are depicted in a relatively fleeting manner or occur during the quite atmospheric sequences which are set during the night. Today they would CGI a film like The Beast Must Die to within an inch of its life and probably lose half of the charm on offer here. The central idea of the film, that one of the guests is really a werewolf but must hide that fact, is always more interesting and creepy than the actual 'werewolf' scenes that occur.

The Beast Must Die has a rather eccentric cast and it's always enjoyable to see them together at the dinner table with vast tracts of werewolf information and musings on things like transmogrification entertainingly coming from Peter Cushing's Dr Lundgren courtesy of a bizarre foreign accent. "Ze urge to eat human flesh is uncontrollable," explains Lundgren as they sit around the dinner table. "I'm afraid der iz vorse to come..." I don't know about anyone else but he'd certainly put me off my Crispy Pancakes if he came around for tea. Cushing nonetheless engages and gains sympathy in his usual quiet way and Michael Gambon and Tom Chadbon are both fun just for their ridiculous seventies hair and clothes. The frilly shirts and period trappings form part of the charm of the film now.

The urbane Charles Gray, who lest we forget played Blofeld in Diamonds Are Forever only a few years before this film, is sadly a trifle underused though as Arthur Bennington and mostly just complains about being held against his will by Newcliffe. I think I would have liked a bit more for Anton Diffring to do as Newcliffe's right hand man Pavel too. Diffring spends most of the film in the high-tech surveillance attempting to track the werewolf for his boss. He's also supposed to be from the country where the werewolves originated so is yet another suspect in the film!

The scenes of these characters all together in the mansion are always quite good fun though and I love the moment when the guests are presented with a blood red sauce at dinner, presumably to entice the werewolf into a slip. "Well, if that was dinner, I can't wait for the cabaret!" says Rick Wakeman lookalike Tom Chadbon. Newcliffe deploys various (and not very subtle) methods in the film designed to make one of his guests suddenly sprout fur and grow fangs so there is plenty of riffing on werewolf mythology with the passing around of silver candlesticks and bullets etc. "Money buys things but men shape events!" says Newcliffe, attempting to explain his obsession to nab a pesky werewolf.

A big part of the cult appeal of The Beast Must Die is surely the eccentric and strange performance of Calvin Lockhart as Newcliffe. Lockhart is ridiculously hammy and theatrical and has a habit of suddenly emphasising random words as if he's trying desperately to impart great weight and meaning. It is a slightly odd spectacle at times with this over enunciating Shaft clone attempting to prod a collection of refined British actors into tripping up and turning into a werewolf. Lockhart's earnestly wooden performance and choice range of camp outfits is a winning combination and it's always oddly compelling when he's running around in the woods with his hunting rifle and an outfit that wouldn't look out of place in an episode of Blake's Seven. Despite my affectionate jesting of Lockhart's thesping prowess I do genuinely enjoy his performance in the film and he's always a commanding and rather stylish presence in his black, slightly military style outfits as the guests mince about in a selection of lighter summer clobber and silly hats.

Despite its obvious flaws and rather modest budget, The Beast Must Die is enjoyable nonsense on the whole with a great central premise (I'm amazed to be honest that no one has ever thought of remaking this). This is an entertaining dose of kitsch seventies British horror from Amicus with a host of familiar faces. And no, the first time I watched this I didn't manage to guess correctly who the werewolf was! Watch out for the "werewolf break" and see if you have better luck...

THE BORDERLANDS (2013)

The Borderlands is a 2013 horror film written and directed by Elliot Goldner. This is a found footage film - which may set some alarm bells ringing because we all probably feel as if we've seen a few too many found footage horror films and found most of them to be mediocre. Let's be honest, an awful lot of found footage films are tedious. There are some good ones out there which come as a nice surpise but you have to sift through an awful lot of chaff to get to the wheat.

Found footage films which I find watchable include Troll Hunter, As Above, So Below (this is the found footage film set in the catacombs and tunnels under Paris - it got poor reviews but I had fun with it), [Rec], Cloverfield, The Blair Witch Project (which is obviously the most famous found footage film), and The Last Broadcast (which everyone apart from me seems to hate). The first Paranormal Activity film was also tolerable I suppose. Found footage films are popular for horror filmmakers because you don't need much money to make one. Found footage is certainly not a new genre and has been around for decades but it was the success of Blair Witch which (for better or worse) jumpstarted the whole thing again. As the V/H/S franchise will attest, found footage films remain quite a popular niche in horror.

So, if we HAVE to include a found footage horror film (not exactly an area festooned with British films I'll grant you) in this book, I would probably pick The Borderlands. Even if you do have an aversion to found footage films, The Borderlands (which was called Final Prayer in the United States) is worth a look and certainly one of the better ones. This film is a decent attempt to make a folk/religious horror with some Lovecraftian influences thrown in there for good measure. The basic plot has Brother Deacon (Gordon Kennedy) and Father Mark Amidon (Aidan McArdle) asked by the Vatican to investigate alleged supernatural activity going on in a church in Devon. Technology expert Gray Parker (Robin Hill) also joins the investigation to film everything and set up surveillance equipment. Well, as you might imagine, things gradually get stranger and stranger and it all builds to a chilling conclusion.

While a lot of elements in The Borderlands may seem more than a trifle familiar (strange goings on in a church or supernatural investigations are hardly new in horror films and many found footage films use a supernatural investigation as their premise) this film is genuinely interesting and well acted too. The film does fall into some well worn found footage tropes but, generally, it is more watchable than a lot of films in this genre. Brother Deacon is a likeable and very human central character and Gordon Kennedy and Robin Hill develop some believable chemistry over the course of the film. The film is quite creepy in a Ghost Stories for Christmas sort of way and gradually builds to to an absorbing last act. Found footage films can be hard going at times but this one manages to gradually reel you in and keep you watching. There is nothing amazingly original about the film but it is very competently put together and well cast.

It is the ending that really makes The Borderlands truly memorable. Without this ending the film probably wouldn't have got as much attention (not that it got much attention anyway) or even be in this book. The big twist at the end is a wonderfully nasty and shocking reveal - a memorably terrible fate. It's the sort of ending which lingers in the memory and that's something you can't say about most horror films - especially found footage films. This ending comes quite abruptly in that it takes a sharp turn into something truly horrifying when it dawns on you what is happening. The Borderlands was certainly shrewd in having this ending up its sleeve because without it you probably would have forgotten the film as soon as the credits had rolled. It also subverts expectations in that it doesn't go for ghosts or the supernatural.

One other thing I like about The Borderlands is that it does at least explain why everything is being filmed. With a lot of found footage films it isn't very plausible that someone would film everything - even in the midst of great danger. If you really hate found footage films you might find the Borderlands a bit of a slog but it is worth the effort to get to that ending and the film is likeable enough with a decent amount of wit and plenty of atmosphere. The locations are nice and often spooky and the cast are all very good. The sound effects in this film are also inventive and add to the creeping sense of unease. The Borderlands is not what you would call a classic but it's one of those modern British horror films which turns out to be somewhat better and more interesting than you expect it to be and at a lean (and sensible) 89 minutes it never threatens to seriously outstay its welcome either.

CAPTAIN KRONOS - VAMPIRE HUNTER (1974)

Captain Kronos – Vampire Hunter was written and directed by Brian Clemens. This is a slightly unusual departure for Hammer in that it is a vampire horror film but also a swashbuckler. Hammer didn't really go in for swashbucklers so this film is quite novel in the Hammer library. The film is a lot of fun and although it got a muted reception when it came out, Kronos is now regarded to be something of a cult classic. The story follows the adventures of Captain Kronos (Horst Janson), a professional vampire hunter, as he hunts down bloodsuckers. His assistant is the hunchback Professor Hieronymus Grost (John Cater). You could say that Captain Kronos is sort of like a period version of that Marvel character Blade! If you have any pesky vampire trouble then Captain Kronos is the man to call.

Unlike traditional vampire films, Captain Kronos takes a fairly unique approach to the genre. Instead of relying on the usual vampire folklore, the film presents vampires as a diverse group, each with their own strengths and weaknesses. Captain Kronos employs various methods to combat the vampires, including sunlight, sacred swords, and other traditional vampire-hunting techniques. Captain Kronos – Vampire Hunter is very entertaining and an atypical sort of entry for Hammer. By the early 1970s, Hammer films were starting to be deemed a bit old-fashioned and twee (especially in the wake of American horror films like Night of the Living Dead, The Texas Chainsaw Massacre, and The Exorcist) so you can see Hammer trying some new things around this time - like kung fu, transplanting Dracula into the present day, and being a bit more risque.

Captain Kronos – Vampire Hunter is something different because it is a swashbuckling action film in addition to being a horror picture. It's a shame really that this film never got a sequel because a Captain Kronos franchise would have been a lot of fun. Captain Kronos: Vampire Hunter had its release delayed for two years (it was made in 1972 but only saw the light of day in 1974) and was given zero marketing. No wonder it bombed - which is a shame. Horst Janson impresses as the charismatic and enigmatic Captain Kronos, certainly looking the part of a dashing hero. Supporting actors, such as John Cater as the knowledgeable Professor Grost, add depth and personality to the plot, and there's a wonderfully nasty turn by Ian Hendry as a thug named Terro.

There is also a nice role for Hammer legend Caroline Munro as Carla, the Gypsy girl who Kronos rescues. They of course become lovers in the end. There won't be any pipe and slippers for Kronos though because a vampire hunter's work is never done. The captain won't be settling down with Carla. He's like Bill Bixby in The Incredible Hulk or that dog in The Littlest Hobo. He has to keep moving on. The cinematography in the film effectively captures the eerie atmosphere of the narrative, painting a gloomy yet alluring picture of the Gothic landscape. The fight scenes, in particular, showcase impressive choreography and innovative camera work, injecting energy and tension into the movie. There's a lot of nifty sword play from Kronos.

The makeup and special effects, given the era in which the film was made, are commendable and effectively contribute to the overall ambiance. One of Captain Kronos' biggest strengths lies in its ability to break free from the clichés that often plague vampire movies. The film ingeniously sidesteps the conventional lore and mythology, introducing new ideas and perspectives regarding vampires and their vulnerabilities. Captain Kronos – Vampire Hunter is an enjoyable romp on the whole and something different from the usual Hammer vampire fare. Kronos deserves its status as a cult film and is a very entertaining vampire horror swashbuckler.

CARRY ON SCREAMING (1966)

The Carry On series began in 1958 and released regular films until 1978. It was resurrected in 1992 but that disastrous venture (Carry On Columbus) proved that the series belonged to the fifties and - especially - the sixties and seventies and should probably remain there. The films, produced by Peter Rogers on very modest budgets and directed by the unflappable Gerald Thomas (who often managed to get scenes done with one take to save time and money), span out of the British tradition of saucy seaside postcards and music hall. Double entendres and innuendo.

Though critics were sniffy, British audiences loved the films and they often featured in the top ten domestic box-office hits of the year. The Carry Ons were a uniquely British institution (Peter Rogers was proud of the fact that they didn't use any foreign money to fund them). Like many people, I grew up watching the Carry On films on television and always loved them. The films are just good old fashioned silly fun. One of the secrets of the success behind the series was the familiar stock company of actors that formed around them. Sid James, Kenneth Williams, Charles Hawtrey, Joan Sims, Hattie Jacques, Peter Butterworth, Kenneth Connor etc.

These performers were not out and out comedians but rather good actors who had the ability to play comedy. It was an important distinction and the reason why they were chosen. The problem with a lot of comedians is that they can't act.

Take someone like Peter Cook for example. He was a brilliantly funny man on chat shows and in comedy sketches but if you put him in a film he couldn't act to save his life. Only the James Bond series can really claim to trump the Carry Ons when it comes to longevity. One can still find the Carry Ons on television to this day, winning new generations of fans. Some of the films are better than others but the Carry Ons are fascinating to explore as they move from Ealingesque black and white to colourful historical parodies to the more risque seventies.

Carry On Screaming was released in 1966. In the Edwardian era, Detective Sergeant-Bung (Harry H Corbett) has to investigate a rash of missing people. The prime suspect is Dr Watt (Kenneth Williams), the strange owner of Bide-A-Wee Rest Home. The Carry Ons spoof Hammer Studios to good effect in Carry On Screaming in this fondly remembered outing for the team. While the Carry Ons are generally remembered as being cheap and cheerful (and I suppose many of them were in their own charming way) we shouldn't forget the craft and invention that went into the historical capers and Carry On screaming serves as an impressive pastiche of Hammer and horror films in general with great cinematography, plenty of atmosphere and some wonderful sets and costumes.

The monsters (which include riffs on The Mummy, Frankenstein's Monster and vampires) are a lot of fun too. Sid James was unavailable to film this one and was replaced by Steptoe & Son star Harry H Corbett (in what would be his only Carry On). Corbett makes a nice addition to the team here and works very well with Peter Butterworth as a comical Holmes & Watson. Fenella Fielding vamps it up as Valaria Watt and Kenny Williams is his usual unrestrained self as the mysterious Dr Watt. He has another memorable much quoted line ("Frying tonight!") near the end. The film riffs not just on Hammer but also The Addams Family television show.

Charles Hawtrey doesn't have an awful lot to do here but Jim

Dale, Joan Sims and Bernard Bresslaw all have their moments. Look out for another Jon Pertwee cameo too. This specific Carry On era was very into the pastiche of particular film genres and historical periods and Carry On Screaming is a great example, falling not too far behind Carry On Cleo in the pantheon of Carry On's period adventures. This is a fairly handsome production by Carry On standards and an affectionate riff on horror films in Carry On style.

CENSOR (2021)

Censor was directed and co-written by Prano Bailey-Bond. It was based on a short film called Nasty which Bailey-Bond had directed. Censor concerns Enid Baines (Niamh Algar), a young woman who works for the British Board of Film Classification in 1985. Enid has to watch endless films to decide what should be cut out or if the film should even be allowed a certificate. The films she has to watch obviously include a lot of low-budget horror and exploitation pictures.

This was the height of the 'video nasty' panic where many horror films became like a sort of forbidden fruit and could be seized and destroyed if they were deemed to be obscene or likely to corrupt. This censorship and tabloid hysteria all seems a bit silly from a modern perspective (especially as horror is fairly mainstream today and gore and blood isn't a big deal) - although one can obviously agree that a certificate system is sensible and you shouldn't allow literally anything to be put in a film.

The remarkable thing about the video nasty era from a modern perspective is that some classic films actually got caught up, to varying degrees, in the video nasty affair. Films like Phantasm, The Texas Chainsaw Massacre, The Evil Dead, The Thing, George Romero's Martin. Basically then, some of the greatest horror films ever made! Anyway, in the film Censor, Enid is having a tough time because a film she approved for release has been linked in the media to a real life murder.

This is something which has happened in real life too. Films like Child's Play and Severance were alleged to have inspired awful and tragic real life crimes. One could probably suggest though that coal-hearted people who lack any conscience, empathy, or compassion, and have no sense of right and wrong (and so are capable of doing dreadful things) would probably do something dreadful in the end even if Child's Play and Severance didn't exist.

Enid is getting abusive phone calls in the story and she's also haunted by a mystery relating to her sister Nina. We see that Enid's parents have registered Nina as legally dead but Enid seems to think that Nina is alive. Enid is then drawn into a mystery when she views some films by cult exploitation director Frederick North (Adrian Schiller). Enid becomes convinced that one of the actors in the films is her supposed dead sister Nina and resolves to go and rescue Nina - who she presumes is some sort of hostage held by these low-budget filmmakers.

Censor is an incredibly stylish film that recreates a grubby realistic version of the 1980s rather than a retro neon fantasy. The offices that Enid works in are very bland and dingy. One interesting thing about Censor is that it doesn't become the sort of film that you expect it to be. You think you can guess where we are heading but the film anticipates this and goes off in another direction - becoming a lot more dreamlike (or nightmarelike if you prefer) than you expected. This seemed to irritate some people but I enjoyed the direction Censor took in the end.

One thing I really love about the film is the way that the aspect ratio gradually changes to resemble a VHS tape from the 1980s. It's a clever touch. There's a fascinating look too at video shop culture in the 1980s where 'video nasties' are kept under the counter as a sort of contraband lest they should be seized by the authorities. It's amazing how times have changed. Take a film like The Burning for example - which was cut to ribbons by the BBFC and then declared a video nasty when a version was put out by someone uncut. You can watch The Burning most weeks on the Horror channel these days. The idea that this film would corrupt or damage anyone seems preposterous today.

Censor is powered by an amazing performance from Niamh Algar as Enid. Algar shines in the central part here and really carries the film. The film has fun with the concept of exploitation filmmaking with this famed underground director making some horror film in the woods and acting as if he's Orson welles or something. Michael Smiley has fun too in his part as a sleazy producer although his encounter with Enid at his house seems like a tonal lurch into more throwaway horror - though this was doubtless deliberate. There aren't that many familiar faces in the cast aside from Nicholas Burns, who plays one of the other censors. Burns has been in everything from Nathan Barley to Black Mirror.

There's a great score by Emilie Levienaise-Farrouch and a perfect sense of detail from seedy offices to rain lashed streets to moonlit woodland. Some people don't like the ending of this film but I thought it was very effective - hypnotic even. Censor is one of the best looking of the modern British horror films and spins a compelling yarn of madness and memory against a backdrop of this strange moral panic inspired by a lot of low-budget horror films.

One of the themes of Censor is our need to find scapegoats for why society isn't what we want it to be. Deciding that society's problems can be connected to some trashy slasher films made on a micro-budget is plainly absurd. Censor is clever in the way that it weaves its story around this fascinating era and uses the video nasty panic and horror films in general in a meta and compelling way. This is one of the best modern British horror films and worth watching for Niamh Algar's performance alone.

THE CITY OF THE DEAD (1960)

The City of the Dead was directed by John Llewellyn Moxey and written by George Baxt. This isn't an official Amicus film but it might as well be. It was produced by Max Rosenberg and Milton Subotsky under their production company Vulcan (this was the only film made under that banner). A few years later they took the name Amicus and the rest is history. The City of the Dead is really more or less an Amicus film. More than that though, The City of the Dead is a brilliant little horror film that deserves to be much better known. If this film was made by Hammer it would be a cult classic.

The City of the Dead was made in Britain (at Shepperton) but is set in the United States. Which would explain why Christopher Lee is grappling with an American accent! The script started life as a pilot for a proposed Boris Karloff television series but this show obviously didn't transpire in the end. The City of the Dead was released in the United States in 1961 under the (rather silly) title Horror Hotel. The American version of The City of the Dead suffered some cuts by the censors and was missing some key scenes.

The story begins in 1692. A witch named Elizabeth Selwyn is burned at the stake but summons supernatural powers to save herself. "In 1692, Elizabeth Selwyn went to the stake, she was buried in the churchyard in New England, and yet 3 years later, 3 years later a new wave of blood sacrifices broke out in the village that condemned her. The daughters of the elders who had condemned her were themselves found dead with every single drop of blood drained from their bodies, and afterwards people came forward to testify that they had actually seen Elizabeth Selwyn." This is a great sequence and very vivid and horrific. The City of the Dead often manages to convey a feverish dream/nightmare atmosphere where we can't always be sure what is real or not. Despite the fact that it was made in 1959, The City of the Dead uses many techniques that feel very modern. You get 'jump scares' and a nice amping up of tension at times.

After the prologue, we go back to the present day where Nan Barlow (Venetia Stevenson) is a curious and attentive student who studies witchcraft in the classes of Professor Alan Driscoll (Christopher Lee). I don't remember A'Level witchcraft at school! I would definitely have taken that class. Nan is persuaded by Driscoll to visit a Massachusetts town called Whitewood that has a long and dark history when it comes to witchcraft and alleged witches. Nan is told that she can learn a lot more about the history of witchcraft in Whitewood and gain some valuable knowledge to prepare herself for her exams. So, Nan travels to this out of the way little town and settles into the Raven's Inn. However, the eccentric owner Mrs Newless (Patricia Jessel) and the locals seem more than a little strange. There is something very weird about this town - as Nan will discover for herself.

The City of the Dead is a beautiful looking horror film with the black and white photography and smoke billowed anachronistic village. This film really does look amazing at times. It's like an episode of The Twilight Zone crossed with Night of the Living Dead. As Nan gets closer and closer to Whitead, the landscape becomes ever more nightmarish and mist shrouded. We begin to develop an unease. No good can come of this visit to Whitewood, we strongly suspect. Maybe it's because it was made around the same time as the first season of Rod Serling's Twilight Zone and also uses black and white and modest studio sets, but The City of the Dead really does feel like watching an elongated 'lost' Twilight Zone episode at times.

It's hard to go into depth with the plot without giving everything away but it is remarkable all the same how much this film is like Psycho (which was released a few months before The City of the Dead but actually went production a month LATER than this film). Both films have an identical structure in the way that they make you think a certain person is the main character and then completely flip that assumption on its head in shocking fashion. Both films then have similar second and third acts with family/friends investigating a disappearance and they even have a similar shocking 'rocking chair' reveal. It's incredible how these two films seem to be so similar in their structure.

This is arguably the scariest film that Rosenberg and Subotsky ever made and has some genuinely tense and creepy moments of horror. You genuinely fear for the characters in The City of the Dead. You should beware of the shorter American cut of this film that is still floating around. That version omits the witch burning scene at the start, presumably because it was deemed too shocking for the censors at the time. This scene is not only very arresting though but segues into the class being taught by Professor Driscoll. It's a very fun theatrical sequence of horror and feels like it should always be a part of the film.

Christopher Lee's American accent is passable enough (even if he doesn't seem entirely comfortable with it) and his performance is commanding enough too for the part. The director has some striking close ups of Lee looking stern and sinister in the film. Venetia Stevenson, who retired from acting not long after The City of the Dead, is likeable enough as the young student. Her performance in this film isn't widely appreciated (it seems - from retrospective reviews) but I like her slightly mannered accent and down to earth nature. Patricia Jessel adds some flamboyance to the cast and Dennis Lotis and Tom Naylor are serviceable enough when they take on more of a central role in the story.

One might argue though that the first half of The City of the Dead is stronger as we learn more about the town through the window of Venetia Stevenson's character. Like her, we get drips and drabs of information and begin to suspect that something is very wrong about this place. The mythology of the story in the film is the sort of thing that The Blair Witch Project traded on. There are some very effective scenes in the film where Nan seems to hear voices and music and evidence of a party but is only met with an empty quiet room when she investigates or tries to join the fun. These scenes are very effective in conveying the strange nature of Whitehood, a place where reality and nightmares seem to be merging into one. The City of the Dead is a great looking and effective horror film that is still very enjoyable. Rarely have fog machines and low budget sets been made to look so striking and chilling.

A CLOCKWORK ORANGE (1971)

A Clockwork Orange was released in 1971 and adapted by Stanley Kubrick from the 1962 Anthony Burgess fable about the choice between good and evil. This is the most infamous of Kubrick's films because it was banned in Britain for many years - its mystique and notoriety of course reaching near legendary proportions because it was forbidden fruit and largely unseen in the country where it was made. The film provoked something of a media storm when it first appeared and was interpreted by some as a celebration of how great it is to be bad. When there were stories of copycat violence and a judge branded it a wicked film, Kubrick asked Warner Bros not to distribute the film in Britain anymore.

He never really explained if he was genuinely disturbed by the effect the film might be having on some troubled souls or if he was just sick to death of all the attention. Maybe it was a combination of the two. The surprising thing about A Clockwork Orange when you do finally watch it is that there appears to be only one onscreen death (it's a novel one though) and the film is of course slightly tamed by the passage of time. But there is definitely a bit of wickedness about A Clockwork Orange, the violence all the more surreal and striking for being wrapped up in the usual spectrum of cinematic effects that is the trademark of Kubrick.

The film centres around Alex (Malcolm McDowell), a Beethoven obsessed teen in a dystopian future Britain who is fond of fighting, rape and murder, and is leader of a small gang known as droogs. A night on the tiles with little Alex can get very obstreperous indeed. Droog chic is white shirt, braces, bowler hat, and a spider web of mascara eyelashes. A composite and tribute to myriad British youth cults from down the decades. They drink milk spiked with hallucinogens and their idea of a good night out is breaking into a house and beating someone up while crooning Gene Kelly's Singin' in the Rain. "The Korova milkbar sold milk-plus, milk plus vellocet or synthemesc or drencrom, which is what we were drinking. This would sharpen you up and make you ready for a bit of the old ultraviolence."

Burgess invented a language called Nadsat that is used by the characters in the film to good effect. Basically a mixture of corrupted Russian (maybe Burgess thought the Russians would win the Cold War) and Cockney rhyming slang. "It's funny how the colours of the real world only seem really real when you viddy them on the screen." A heady cocktail of slapstick and violence ensues but two of the other droogs Dim (Warren Clarke) and Georgie (James Marcus) become resentful of his leadership and decide to frame him for a crime. He is convicted to 14 years in prison and becomes a subject for a government experimental rehabilitation scheme (Ludovico Technique - a kind of aversion therapy that causes him to retch at the mere thought of violence or sex). Can they transform the psychopathic delinquent into a politically correct and safe human being? And does the state have the right to remove free will? A remarkably dangerous and frightening tool in the hands of a totalitarian government.

I read A Clockwork Orange once on a train journey between Victoria station and Canterbury and it's a short but vivid and compelling book. Burgess' wife was raped by American deserters during the war and he later witnessed the first battle between Mods and Rockers on Brighton seafront so one can see where the inspiration for the book came from. This is a moderately faithful adaption although Kubrick of course always puts his own stamp on whatever project he directs, no matter who was behind the source material. Arthur C Clarke,

Stephen King, Anthony Burgess or whoever. It seems to me that the most salient differences are the inversion of the ending and Kubrick's tendency to add a whiff of glamour and beauty to the violence.

The book was violent too but maybe the Nadsat narration took the edge off. Kubrick, to be fair, has to show things, not describe them. This was perhaps the thing that made the film so controversial. The symphonic beauty of the violence, as choreographed and visually striking as a dance number in a Hollywood musical. A Clockwork Orange is a film that seems to almost enjoy its dirty deeds. One of the surprising things about the film when you watch it for the first time though is that the droog "ultraviolence" is confined only to the first section of the film. Maybe twenty, twenty five minutes or something. Thereafter Alex is a victim, covered in snot and in prison.

One tends to immediately conjure images of the mascara bowler hatted teen hijinks when you think of A Clockwork Orange but it's only a small part of the story. Maybe the film loses something at some point with this shift (Kubrick has less scope for fantastic visual flourishes) but it always remains interesting and relatively compelling. Malcolm McDowell, for all the evil deeds of his character, remains a strangely likeable and seductive anti-hero, referring to us - the audience - as "my brothers" as he narrates this terrible tale. It's a great performance and he has definite charisma. It captures him at his best before he got older and began to slip into role of stock Hollywood nutty villain like a comfortable pair of slippers.

You can see the influence of Alex in a range of characters. Even Heath Ledger's Joker. I love the classical music selections and synthesiser compositions by Wendy Carlos and there is clever use of Beethoven's 9th Symphony, The William Tell Overture, and of course and most shockingly, Singin' in the Rain. A stylised gang fight occurs beneath the strains of Rossini's The Thieving Magpie. The Thamesmead estate in London makes a striking backdrop in the first portion of the film. Brutal futuristic architecture that sort of looks beautiful and depressing at the same time.

Kubrick uses Thamesmead for one of the most memorable flourishes in the film where Alex thrashes a couple of his droogs for hinting at mutiny and one ends up in the water. A simple scene but the use of slow motion and music makes it somehow epic. Look for some familiar faces in the supporting cast. Steven Berkoff, the wonderful and barking mad Patrick Magee as Frank Alexander - the writer whose house Alex and his droogs break into. Oh, and David (Darth Vader) Prowse in a pair of pants. A Clockwork Orange is a difficult film but a great one at its best and an essential part of the Kubrick mythology.

THE COMPANY OF WOLVES (1984)

The Company of Wolves was directed by Neil Jordan and is based on the short story collection The Bloody Chamber by Angela Carter. This is one of those films which deserves to be more famous than it ever was. The story revolves around a young girl named Rosaleen, played by Sarah Patterson, who has weird dreams of being chased by wolves. Set in a remote village, the film explores various tales of werewolves and the dangerous nature of men. The film intertwines different fantastical stories that delve into themes of sexuality, transformation, and the power of storytelling. The Company of Wolves incorporates elements from various fairy tales and myths to explore deeper psychological and symbolic meanings. It subverts traditional fairy tale structures and uses them to reflect the darker aspects of human nature.

The Company of Wolves features striking visual design, offering hypnotic cinematography that enhances its eerie, otherworldly atmosphere. The lush forest landscapes and intricately designed costume and set pieces create a palpable sense of dread and mystique. The film's intricate and vivid production design heightens the dreamlike quality, constantly blurring the line between fantasy and reality. Sarah Patterson (who didn't seem to do much acting after this film) captures the innocence and curiosity of Rosaleen's character and Angela Lansbury delivers a nice performance as Rosaleen's wise and mischievous grandmother, who guides her through the dark and twisted tales.

Sarah Patterson, according to her date of birth on Wikipedia, would only have been about fourteen when this film came out so it's a great performance for someone so young. There are a raft of familiar faces in the film like David Warner, Stephen Rea, and Brian Glover. The Company of Wolves is one of the most dreamlike films you will ever watch. It is almost like a sort of anthology too in the way it weaves in different stories that are loosely connected. This film is probably not going to be everyone's cup of tea but it is a unique experience and something everyone should watch at least once.

There is truly nothing else quite like The Company of Wolves and the ambition of the film is laudable on what must have been a relatively modest budget. For some reason this is one of those films that is rarely on television so it has been a trifle forgotten over the years but it is definitely a film that all British horror fans should experience.

The Company of Wolves offers a different sort of take on the werewolf genre and is an engagingly trippy and fantastical experience at times. The film is sort of like a rich pudding where you wouldn't want to eat too much of it but at 95 minutes you can enjoy the pudding without getting too full and sick of it.

A big strength of The Company of Wolves is that the film challenges and subverts traditional narrative structures, questioning the expectations and conventions of storytelling. It explores the power of dreams as a reflection of our fears, desires, and subconscious thoughts. The Company of Wolves only cost about £2 million to make but it has incredible animatronic werewolf effects and recreated a fairytale forest at Shepperton Studios. It is an amazing feat of production given that they had so little money up their sleeve.

The Company of Wolves can probably best be described as an arthouse horror fairytale. A film like this today would be full of digital backdrops and CGI effects. It just wouldn't be the same at all. The fact that The Company of Wolves was made in the early 1980s with old school effects and sets makes it all the more charming from a modern vantage point.

CORRUPTION (1968)

Corruption was directed by Robert Hartford-Davis. The film stars Peter Cushing as Sir John Rowan, a renowned surgeon, and Sue Lloyd as Lynn Nolan, his much younger fiancée. Lynn works as a fashion model and while being photographed at some Swinging Sixties style party, Rowan, increasingly irritated by the risque nature of the photographs being taken of Lynn, gets into a fight with a photographer. I can't say I blame Dr Rowan here. The people at the party are insufferable and treat him like some doddery old fossil.

In the resulting chaos caused by this fracas, a lamp falls on Lynn and badly disfigures her face - ruining her looks. She feels as if her life is ruined but Rowan devises a way to restore her looks using a glandular extract from the glands of corpses. There is only one problem though - and it's a big problem at that. The effect is only temporary. Dr Rowan needs fresh corpses from time to time. Rowan will have to resort to murder on a fairly regular basis if he wants to maintain Lynn's looks.

This is a fairly obscure British horror film but it is a lot fun. It's probably the closest we ever got to seeing Peter Cushing in a British style Grindhouse exploitation film. Corruption is a lot sleazier and violent than the Amicus and Hammer films and

Cushing's character, who is refined and gentle at the start, has to become a crazed serial killer because he will literally do anything to please his much younger girlfriend. It's a story of obsession.

They say there's no fool like an old fool and that's definitely the case with Dr Rowan. He will do anything for Lynn - even commit murder. Lynn is as much the villain of the piece as Rowan. Rowan becomes an unhinged lunatic but he is at least aware that what he is doing is wrong. In the end he becomes reluctant to kill but if he doesn't he will lose Lynn. He can't win whatever he does. There is a decent amount of tension in the film and the scene where Rowan decides to murder a prostitute is very compelling. At times the film plays a bit like that Hitchcock film Frenzy (though Corruption is obviously not as polished and inventive as Frenzy).

The start of the film is interesting because you have this clash of generations. Dr Rowan is completely out of his element at the madcap Swinging Sixties party and seems like he's just wandered in from another century. The film has some nice beach scenes near the end and it is compelling when Rowan and Lynn take in a young girl named Terry (Wendy Varnals) as a potential victim. The home invasion stuff at the end feels somewhat silly and generic and the ending might feel a cop-out to some but, generally, this film is bizarre enough to be very entertaining and it is something a bit different from all the Gothic and period British horror films which abounded in this era.

By the way, there are some very familiar faces with small roles in this film. Anthony Booth (the 'Scouse git' from Alf Garnett) is the annoying smug photographer at the party and this sequence also features the legendary Vanessa Howard as a ditsy young woman. As ever, Howard steals the scene she is in. Corruption may not be as well-known as other films of the era but has gained a modest cult following over the years for its unique blend of horror and crime elements. The film features fairly graphic scenes of violence and gore for the time (though they've obviously been tamed by the passage of time), characteristic of the exploitation films of the late 1960s. It is certainly fun to see Cushing in a slightly different type of horror film. Corruption is not what you would describe as a lost classic but it is a lot of fun and very watchable.

THE CURSE OF FRANKENSTEIN (1957)

The Curse of Frankenstein is a Hammer film, loosely based on the 1818 novel Frankenstein by Mary Shelley. * It was Hammer's first colour horror film and the first of their (many) Frankenstein pictures. The film was directed by Terence Fisher and written by Jimmy Sangster. The story in this screen adaptation is framed by Baron Victor Frankenstein (Peter Cushing) in prison awaiting execution for the murder of his maid Justine. He tells a priest (Alex Gallier) what really happened - the maid was killed by a monster (Christopher Lee) he created. The 'monster' was supposed to be highly intelligent, a man brought back to life using various body parts, but the brain was damaged and the creature was unpredictable and violent. Although the priest doesn't believe him we see this tale play out in flashbacks.

This is not the most faithful adaptation of Frankenstein but it is a lot of fun. They obviously had to be careful not to mimic the Universal versions so the monster makeup is very different here and the film does its own thing rather than ape what has gone before. This was apparently helped by the fact that Jimmy Sangster had never seen any other versions of Frankenstein and so just used the book instead. A lot of stuff from the novel was jettisoned because they simply didn't have the money to adapt everything. The Curse of Frankenstein is a fairly short film so it cuts straight to the chase and doesn't drag at all.

I love Peter Cushing as Victor Frankenstein because he plays him as a very cultured man who is often snotty towards others because he deems them inferior. You get the impression that Cushing had fun playing a brilliant but arrogant man like Victor. Melvin Hayes plays the young Victor before Cushing takes over. Robert Urquhart is good as Paul Krempe, the tutor who becomes Victor's assistant but eventually becomes troubled by the ethics of their research. Hazel Court is also very good in the film as Elizabeth. Christopher Lee naturally makes a fine monster (billed as the 'Creature' in the credits) and the fact Lee was 6'5 in height and towers over everyone else obviously helps to make the monster seem intimidating.

The blood in the film was quite shocking at the time given this was Hammer's first colour film - though naturally this shock factor has long since been dulled by the passage of time. Like all the early Hammer colour films, there is something wonderfully cosy and familiar about this picture which means you can watch it over and over again. By the way, it was apparently Max Rosenberg who came to Hammer with the idea of doing a Frankenstein film and he even gave them a script by Milton Subotsky. Rosenberg claimed that Hammer stiffed him out of a profit share deal for this film and just gave him a modest flat fee. This, presumably, is what motivated Rosenberg and Subotsky to set up Amicus Films - who became Hammer's main British horror rival. If this story is true you could say that Amicus Films was, to use a Curb Your Enthusiasm reference, a spite store!

* Frankenstein was written by Mary Shelley when she was only eighteen years-old. Frankenstein is a pioneering work of science fiction and an enduring touchstone of horror. To this day, rarely a year goes past without a film that was inspired by Frankenstein going into production. It is hard to think of any work of fiction that has been as influential as Frankenstein was to the horror genre. The book was written in 1818 while Mary was staying a villa near Geneva close to Lord Byron. The story was, appropriately enough, inspired by a nightmare.

The story in Frankenstein is told through the letters of an explorer named Captain Robert Walton. Walton is on an exploration of the North Pole and runs into a mysterious and cultivated Swiss scientist named Victor Frankenstein. Frankenstein has discovered a way to bring life to body parts that were previously dead. He has meddled with things that shouldn't really have been meddled with at all. The end result is the creation of a monster who inspires fear but only wants to be loved and accepted. We are faced with the realisation that the real monster may not be this unfortunate creature but Victor Frankenstein himself.

Even if you've never read Frankenstein before you might feel as if you are already familiar with this story. The mad scientist, a lightning crackled gothic laboratory, villagers with pitchforks and flaming torches. However, if that's the case you will be surprised at how the original novel subverts your expectations. This book is a lot different to how one might expect it to be from watching Frankenstein movies. The story is more complex, much bigger, more nuanced, and simply a lot more surprising than any film verson you might have seen. As a consequence, Frankenstein feels like a fresh and (ahem) novel experience which is completely different to what you expected. This is one of the true landmarks and cornerstones of the horror genre but also a very moving and very human story.

DEADLY STRANGERS (1975)

A 1975 British psychological thriller directed by Sidney Hayers, Deadly Strangers plays like a good episode of Hammer House of Mystery and Suspense and doesn't deserve its relative obscurity. The film begins with a violent escape from a lunatic asylum but we don't see who it was that escaped. Steven (Simon Ward) is a salesman driving around in an Austin Maxi who picks up a young woman named Belle (Hayley Mills) in the rain after she was attacked by a lorry driver who gave her a lift.

Steven, who seems to be a peeping Tom, lies about the last

train having gone so that she will ride with him and keep him company while the prim Belle seems to hiding secrets. Both seem like lost souls tormented by the past. The pair end up driving around the West Country as the secrets they hold come ever more slowly to the surface and the police begin to dog them after Steven runs an annoying motorcyclist off the road. Well, suffice to say, we'll find out who it was who escaped from that asylum before the end credits roll.

You'll probably work out the ending long before we arrive but this a generally absorbing little film with a nice sense of atmosphere. It seems to have been shot in the countryside and by the seaside in the winter (Bristol and Somerset were apparently the main locations) and the grotty film quality and muted colours add to the ambiance. This is a very 1970s example of a British film. It looks like it cost no money to make, there are greasy spoon motorway cafes (look how much fat the cook uses when he fries that egg!), rubbish motorcycle ruffians in leather jackets, and hotel owners that get irritated when they have a customer.

Simon Ward feels slightly miscast as the socially inept Steven but it's interesting to see former Disney star Hayley Mills in a more adult role. She would have been nearly thirty at the time and dropped out of the film business after this for many years. Mills has a nude scene and has to fend off the unwelcome attentions of Peter Jeffrey as her sleazy childhood guardian in flashbacks. The primness she brings to the part suits the character and helps the story.

Look out too for a bizarre cameo by Sterling Hayden as a man in a vintage sports car who tries to woo Belle. Hayden has an eccentric beard and ends up chasing them around a multi storey car park. Believe it or not, Hayden turned down the part of the shark hunter Quint in 1975's Jaws but DID agree to appear in Deadly Strangers that same year. That seems like a bizarre career move but I suppose to be fair to Hayden he had no idea that Jaws was going to be such a blockbuster. So, instead of appearing in one of the most famous films ever made and delivering that USS Indianapolis speech for Steven Spielberg, Hayden instead walked up and down the Grand Pier in Weston super Mare with Hayley Mills in freezing cold weather.

The direction is no great shakes and the film looks rather drab but it does hold your attention once you've settled into it and Deadly Strangers is worth sticking with to the end. It's no Frenzy but it is an interesting little thriller that gets you hooked. The opening scenes are very atmospheric and creepy and Ward and Mills, to their credit, give earnest performances and take the material seriously. One good thing about Deadly Strangers too is that at 88 minutes it doesn't stretch out its premise too far and threaten to outstay its welcome. With a few edits I think this would have made a very decent episode of one of the Hammer 1980s television shows.

DEAD OF NIGHT (1945)

Dead of Night is a classic and highly influential 1945 British portmanteau horror film by Ealing Studios featuring stories directed by Alberto Cavalcanti, Charles Crichton, Basil Dearden and Robert Hamer. The film begins with architect Walter Craig (Mervyn Johns) arriving at a country house where a number of guests are waiting. Walter immediately has a strange and powerful sense of deja vu and feels like he has been here in this same situation before. He explains, to a rather dubious audience, that each of them is part of a nightmare he is having and predicts an event that soon happens to try and prove his point. Everyone is soon intrigued, except for psychiatrist Dr Van Straaten (Frederick Valk).

"Well, if I am a puppet and Mr Craig's pulling the strings, the least he can do is to tell me a little bit more about the part he's giving me to play," says the doctor. "I wish it were as easy as that," replies Walter. "But trying to remember a dream is like, how shall I put it, being out at night in a thunder-storm.

There's a flash of lightning and, for one brief moment, everything stands out: vivid and startling." We return to the country house and the various characters debating Walter's suggestion throughout the film and his confession induces them to talk about their own strange experiences. In horror anthology tradition we see the experiences they relate in the form of short stories all linked by the guests in the country house...

The first story - The Hearse Driver - was directed by Basil Dearden from a story by E. F. Benson. "Well, when it comes to foreseeing the future," says racing driver Hugh Gainger (Anthony Baird) to Dr Van Straaten in the country house. "Something once happened to me that knocks your theories into a cocked hat. Something I'll not forget to my dying day." In Hugh's story we begin with him recovering in hospital after a crash and the dapper sporting hero is soon charming his nurse. One night though, Hugh wakes up in the middle of night and decides to read a book for a while. He's rather perturbed to see daylight outside and, more worryingly, an anachronistic horse-drawn hearse and the driver (Miles Malleson) looking at him. "Just room for one inside, sir," says the hearse driver cheerfully to Hugh. Grainger goes back to bed and eventually shrugs it off as a dream or delusion but, in this tale of premonition, the dream will come back to haunt him. Despite a simple and slight set-up, The Hearse Driver is expertly handled with a nice twist in the tale that will cause a few chills. Dead of Night has a nice offbeat and supernatural air throughout - a sort of film within a dream feeling - and The Hearse Driver is a good example of this.

The next story is The Christmas Story and was directed by Alberto Cavalcanti. At a Christmas party in an old spacious house, young Sally (Sally Ann Howes) plays hide and seek and has a nice time but an obstreperous scamp enjoys telling Sally that the house is haunted because of an old murder that occurred way back in 1860. Sally later stumbles across a sobbing boy at the top of a hidden flight of stairs (which will soon be disconcertingly elusive) who tells her that unspeakable threats are being made to him. She consoles the boy and returns to the party but Sally is about to get a very unsettling surprise. A ridiculously simple premise is used to wonderfully eerie effect in this story with the black and white adding to the weird and wonderfully anachronistic atmosphere. Though a little mawkish at times, this story is fantastically ghostly and British and does have a suitably spooky twist that is very creepy.

The next tale is The Haunted Mirror, directed by Robert Hamer from a story by John V. Baines. Joan (Googie Withers) buys a Victorian mirror from an antique shop for her fiance Peter (Ralph Michael) but when Peter uses the mirror he has a vague impression that the reflection he sees doesn't match his own surroundings and eventually becomes withdrawn and bad tempered. The 'visions' are starting to affect Peter greatly and when Joan forces him to look in the mirror with her he sees a strange Victorian scene and an ornate bedroom with a log fire. "But in a queer sort of way, it fascinates me," says Peter of the mirror. "I feel as though that room, the one in the mirror, were trying to... to claim me. To draw me into it. It almost becomes the real room, and my own bedroom imaginary." Joan naturally suspects her fiancée might be going completely mad but a visit to the antique shop reveals the true origin and secret of the mirror. A strong segment and clearly an influence on similar spooky mirror shenanigans with David Warner in the seventies Amicus compendium From Beyond the Grave. This story pulls you in as things become ever more strange and Ralph Michael does a decent job as the spooky reflections in the mirror eventually begin to threaten Peter's sanity.

The next offering is The Golfing Story directed by Charles Crichton. It stars Basil Radford and Naunton Wayne as rival golfers George and Larry, forever feuding on the golf course but otherwise good friends. George and Larry's friendship is threatened however when Mary (Peggy Bryan) can't choose between them. They decide, as you do, to play eighteen holes of golf for her, with the loser to be a decent chap and disappear... permanently. "The loser to vanish from the scene," says George. The triumphant George wins the prize but will Larry let him enjoy it? Perhaps the weakest link in the film, The Golfing Story is a fairly jovial jape and seems a tad out of place in the film as a whole but it is quite likeable nonetheless and serves as a sort of spoof of glossy 'afterlife' films. It's quite amusing at times ("Cheat! Cad! Twister! May the Lord have mercy on your handicap!") and the set-up, play golf, loser commits suicide, is fairly dark despite the whimsical nature of the piece.

The final and most famous story in Dead of Night is The Ventriloquist's Dummy, directed by Cavalcanti again and featuring Michael Redgrave as nutty ventriloquist Maxwell Frere.

Maxwell's major problem is that he is becoming increasing dominated by his dummy Hugo which is, it has to be said, a bit scary and not the most pleasant character. Under the growing influence of this creepy puppet, things are only going to go from bad to worse for Maxwell. The Ventriloquist's Dummy has been done subsequent times since Dead of Night came out, from Magic with Anthony Hopkins to Child's Play, but the copycats have yet to diminish the more vintage chills supplied here. Michael Redgrave is really good in this segment as the nervous, twitchy ventriloquist rapidly heading for a nervous breakdown and there is a scary final scene to wrap things up. I like too the depiction of a certain boozy low-rent post-war showbusiness world where people are struggling to get by as the country tries to get back on its feet again. This story is very creepy and there are some genuinely unsettling moments, especially when Hugo suddenly starts talking to American ventriloquist Sylvester Kee (Hartley Power) without Maxwell or we get the warning "You don't know what Hugo's capable of..."

We then return to the country house and the final wrap-up which is very eerie, incorporating all the stories and continuing the dreamlike atmosphere of the film. The country house banter is good fun on the whole and contains all the characters. I should mention Roland Culver as Eliot Foley, the man who invited them in the first place, who is good value debating with Craig and Van Straaten. Dead of Night is made to feel like a recurring nightmare and the black and white and post-war detail and atmosphere adds a great deal to the ghostly trappings. If you suspect that a British black and white film made way back in 1945 is unlikely to supply any chills today then Dead of Night will prove you wrong. One to watch late at night with the lights off.

DEATH LINE (1972)

Death Line is a British horror film directed by Gary Sherman. It is known as Raw Meat in the United States. What is the premise of Death Line? Students Patricia (Sharon Gurney) and Alex (David Ladd) get off a train at Russell Square tube station late at night and stumble across an unconscious man on the steps. Patricia insists that they get help and - despite the protests of Alex, who thinks the man probably just had too much to drink, they notify the police. However, when they return the man is gone. Inspector Calhoun (Donald Pleasance) investigates and uncovers a most grisly conspiracy from the depths of London...

Death Line has become a cult film over the decades for a number of reasons. The actual mystery is sort of silly (descendants of Victorian workers trapped in tunnels have become cannibals and, now desperate for food, prey on commuters) but it works thanks to the very sympathetic performance of Hugh Armstrong as the (soon to be last) cannibal. Despite the fact that he kills and eats people you feel sorry for him and the pathetic existence he's had to eke out. He was only trying to provide for his ill wife. "Mind the doors!" is the only thing he has learned to say. It's strangely moving witnessing the plight of this deadly savage.

The film is genuinely grisly and bloody at times and that

tracking shot of the cannibal lair is worth the price of admission on its own. The film taps into the alienation and innate strangeness of subway systems very well. In terms of London Underground horror setpieces the only rival Death Line has is An American Werewolf in London. The thing most people remember about the film though is the truly bonkers and hilarious performance of Donald Pleasance as the policeman who has to investigate.

Pleasance seems to be genuinely enjoying himself and makes the tea guzzling Calhoun cynical, sarcastic and irreverent as he dispenses wisecracks and investigates the mystery in a most amusing way. Death Line is one of the finest hours of Donald Pleasance and it wouldn't be nearly as much fun without him. How brilliant would it have been to have some sequels where Calhoun encountered other strange mysteries like a British version of The Night Stalker? Watch out for the short but brilliant scene where Christopher Lee makes a cameo as a snooty MI5 official who warns Calhoun off the case. It's an incredible confrontation conveyed by two great actors. The recurring British obsession with social class is an obvious theme in Death Line.

There's a rich 1970s atmosphere in the film that makes it interesting. The scuzzy Soho sex district at the start, the bohemian students, the bowler hatted commuter. The actors playing the students are fairly forgettable but Pleasance is great and well supported by Norman Rossington as his assistant. Look out for Clive Swift too as Inspector Richardson. Death Line is a unique experience and quite unlike any other horror film you've seen. It's violent, suspenseful, sad, funny, and genuinely strange at times. You'll never look at the London Underground in quite the same way again.

THE DESCENT (2005)

The Descent was directed by Neil Marshall. Who isn't a sucker for a good cave horror film? Lest we forget The Strangeness? Well, ok, let's forget that one. How about the cheekily titled Italian film Alien 2: On Earth - another low-budget shocker which takes place in caves? On second thoughts, let's forget that one too. My Bloody Valentine (the original of course) is great - although it does take a while to actually get underground in that film. The undisputed champion of cave horror films is surely though The Descent - the finest hour of Neil Marshall and one of the finest hours of modern British horror. The Descent is the Citizen Kane of cave themed horror films. That might sound like damning with faint praise but The Descent is very good indeed.

What is the plot of The Descent? A group of women go on a caving expedition in the Appalachian Mountains. Sarah (Shauna Macdonald) was encouraged to go on the expedition as a sort of healing exercise after she lost her husband and daughter in a crash. I must say I don't understand potholing at all as a hobby. Sure, it must be interesting to explore ancient caves but all the money in the world wouldn't get me down in some dark, narrow cave. Once down in the depths of the caves, some tensions and secrets begin to emerge among the group of women in The Descent. That's not all though. As they venture into an unexplored cave system they begin to encounter the real possibility that they might be lost or trapped. They are not alone down there either. There are cave dwelling humanoids who can see in the dark and they aren't especially friendly...

If, like me, you are claustrophobic (I don't even like being inside small cars) then The Descent is one of the most intense film experiences you are ever likely to experience. Those narrow underground cave passages the characters have to crawl through will give you nightmares. This is a very inventive film which makes great use of its constrictive underground location. The film is both atmospheric and gripping and the characters are pretty good too. It probably wouldn't be going completely over the top to say that The Descent is one of the best horror films of the 21st century so far.

There seemed to be no stopping Neil Marshall at the time but - sadly - his film directing career hit the skids with Doomsday and never really recovered again. His last few films have been so bad that it's hard to believe they were made by the same man who gave us Dog Soldiers and The Descent. What went wrong? I have no idea really although Marshall's films suddenly seemed to get worse when he had slightly bigger budgets. Maybe that had something to do with it. Anyway, The Descent is fantastic and the monsters known as 'crawlers' are very creepy. It takes a long time for the monsters to show up. Neil Marshall said he wanted claustrophobia to be the terror and then just when you think things can't get any worse...they do!

The claustrophobia was more than sufficient to make The Descent terrifying for me but the introduction of the 'crawlers' suddenly plunges the film into more overt horror film territory and this is great fun. It was deemed too dangerous to film The Descent in real caves so cave sets were built at Pinewood. The exterior scenes were filmed in Scotland. A portion of the dialogue in The Descent had to be dubbed in later during ADR. This is because the cave sets were fake and therefore when the actors talked it didn't sound like they were in a real cave. The cast in The Descent are all pretty good and it was a lot more rare to have an all female cast in 2005 than it might be today. Some of the cave peril antics will make you shudder in fear. This is a great looking film that is very well made.

A few nitpickers felt the film became a trifle generic when it veered into horror territory with the crawlers but all the horror stuff is good if you ask me and The Descent works as a coherent whole which doesn't have a jarring tonal lurch. The American version of this film famously had a different ending which was slightly more hopeful than the British version. I prefer the British ending but I gather Neil Marshall wasn't too bothered by which ending they went with as he shot several different endings and was happy for any of them to be used. The Descent is not only a great horror film but also an interesting meditation on guilt, grief and friendship. It's just a shame really that Neil Marshall seemed to peak so soon. He's done some great television work but he never really managed to follow through on the promise of his first two films.

DOG SOLDIERS (2002)

Dog Soldiers was directed by Neil Marshall and despite its minuscule budget it has gone on to become a minor cult favourite. The film is set in the Scottish Highlands and begins with a couple camping in the forest. Something unzips their tent and kills them but we don't see what it is. We move onto a squad of British soldiers on a training exercise in the forest. They are led by Sergeant Wells (Sean Pertwee) but we know Kevin McKidd as Private Cooper is going to be the lead because we get a prologue with him where he seems to be trying to pass an SAS endurance test but fails because he refuses to shoot a dog.

So, anyway, the soldiers are in the forest but grumbling because they are missing a big football match. They are spooked when something throws a dead cow at them and then they find the savaged remains of an SAS team they were supposed to be playing wargames against. The survivor Captain Ryan (Liam Cunningham) is an old foe of Cooper from his special forces test and remains vague about what happened to the men in the forest. It transpires that werewolves happened and these pesky werewolves soon start attacking the squad...

I didn't care much for Dog Soldiers when I first watched it but liked it much more on a second viewing. For me anyway, this is one of those films that I came to appreciate more when I watched it again. Dog Soldiers is quite gory in places but could be described as a horror comedy as it has a lot of humour. The film references a lot of stuff, like Predator (Predator is clearly one of the biggest influences on Dog Soldiers), Southern Comfort, Night of the Living Dead, Zulu, The Howling, and so on. The cast are great and believable as army squaddies and there are some decent laughs.

Darren Morfitt steals the show as Private 'Spoon' Witherspoon. Spoon is like the ultra tough gung ho one you always get in these types of films but he's a badass in a very chav British sort of way. Even when he's out of weapons and ammo, Spoons is perfectly happy to take on a werewolf with pots, pans, cutlery and even his fists. It's great fun when the soldiers are being chased through the forest by the werewolves and it's slightly disappointing in a way when they end taking refuge in a farmhouse and it becomes more of a siege film. The farmhouse sequences are very inventive but an air of deja vu hangs over the second act. The soldiers v werewolves in the forest scenes were more enjoyable because Marshall was clearly doing a homage to Predator.

The werewolves are a little on the hokey side as they are basically just actors in suits wearing huge werewolf heads. I suppose the production didn't have the money for any fancy CGI or animatronics. At least it gives the creatures a sense of life and weight though. Dog Soldiers would probably look awful now if they'd used cheap 2002 CGI. Sean Pertwee is great as Wells, the sarge ending up with his guts hanging out and having to resort to superglue. Kevin McKidd, best known for Trainspotting, makes a pretty good lead as Cooper. Jason Statham was supposed to play Cooper but dropped out to make Ghosts of Mars. As good as McKidd is, Dog Soldiers would probably be even more of a cult film now with Statham in the lead.

Dog Soldiers is not an out and out classic but it is a very likeable effort with plenty of invention. It was quite obvious that Neil Marshall would be a name to watch after this. Considering that this film was made on an absolute shoestring its a very decent action horror film and one that has a good sense of humour too. I would have liked a bit more of the soldiers battling the werewolves in the forest but cabin siege portion of the film, despite being a hoary old staple in horror films and VERY familiar, is at least handled with plenty of verve and invention by Marshall.

DON'T LOOK NOW (1973)

Don't Look Now was directed by Nicolas Roeg and adapted from the 1971 short story by Daphne du Maurier. John Baxter (Donald Sutherland) and Laura Baxter (Julia Christie) are a couple still trying to cope with the immense grief and sorrow caused by the death of their young daughter Christine in a drowning accident. John takes a job in Venice restoring an old church but the couple meet two elderly sisters there - one of whom, Heather, claims to be psychic.

Heather claims to have a message from Christine from beyond the grave. Christine wants John to get out of Venice because he is in danger. Laura is shaken by all of this but John is not convinced that Heather is really psychic. However, he soon begins to experience strange occurrences - which suggest he really might be in danger. He also begins to see an image of a child in Venice wearing a red coat - which was what Christine was wearing when she had her accident. What can any of this mean?

Don't Look Now is regarded to be a masterpiece today but it actually got a few sniffy reviews when it came out. The film did very well in Britain (where it featured on a double bill with The Wicker Man - what a double bill that must have been for horror fans!) but not so well in the United States. The status of the film has only grown over the years though and the film has been hugely influential.

One of the interesting devices in the film is the use of editing so that the past, present, and future are fluid and can all exist at the same time. This is used in the premonition scene on the river. The film became quite famous for the bold sex scene - which was so bold many assumed it to be real (which it wasn't). This scene is intercut with John and Laura getting dressed. Nicholas Roeg said he did this to placate the censors. If he'd just included the sex scene in one uninterrupted block the censors would have kicked up more fuss.

Although the film has elements of the supernatural it is essentially about a real life horror - the awful nature of grief and guilt and how it is almost impossible to live with at times. Don't Look Now has two superlative performances from Sutherland and Christie and also offers a different cinematic slant on Venice. We think of Venice as a sunlit place where rich arty people go for weekends to eat posh grub and hobnob on the canals but in Don't Look Now it becomes a sinister, dark and ghostly sort of place. The film's crowning achievement lies in its ability to defy expectations and manipulate viewers' perceptions.

Roeg expertly intertwines various narrative elements, making it impossible to discern what is real and what is imagined. He seamlessly blends moments of disturbing horror with those of intense emotional intimacy, leaving us constantly questioning the boundaries of our own perception. This skillful handling of the supernatural makes Don't Look Now a precursor to psychological thrillers that followed. Don't Look Now also has a truly unforgettable ending - which comes as a real shock the first time you watch the film.

What really makes Don't Look Now special is that it doesn't feel like any other film. It is its own thing and takes the viewer on a strange and compelling journey quite unlike anything else. This is one of those films too which rewards more than one viewing - which is why most of us have probably watched this film more times than we care to remember.

Nicolas Roeg had already put himself on the map with Performance and Walkabout but it was Don't Look Now which catapulted him into cult status. While he never quite hit the heights of Don't Look Now again he would still make some fascinating and striking films - like Bad Timing and The Man

Who Fell to Earth.

DRACULA (1958)

Dracula was directed by Terence Fisher and written by Jimmy Sangster. This was the first of Hammer's Dracula films and it was genius casting to get Christopher Lee for the title role. Because he was a such a commanding and polished presence it only took some contact lenses, a cape and a bit of make-up magic to turn Christopher Lee into a memorable Dracula. Lee said he didn't watch any other Dracula films because he wanted his performance to be original and not influenced by anything else.

Christopher Lee is often credited with being the first actor to make Dracula 'sexy' and bring more of an erotic subtext to Dracula's neck biting shenanigans. Christopher Lee would eventually tire of playing Dracula and by all accounts didn't think too much of the later Dracula pictures by Hammer. He's always great though in this role and, whether he liked it or not, it is what he's remembered for more than anything.

As if that wasn't enough you also - of course - get Peter Cushing as Van Helsing in Dracula. Lee and Cushing are surely the greatest horror double act in history. If these two are in a film you know they are going to 'class' the picture up and make it much better than it might otherwise have been. Even the silliest film becomes instantly watchable if Cushing and Lee are involved. Not to say that Dracula is a silly film though - this is a really good film and the most 'sober' of their Dracula pictures (later on they tried to shake the formula up with lesbians, kung fu, modern day settings etc).

The story is more or less the same in this film as the novel but there are a number of changes in this screen adaptation. Jonathan Harker (John Van Eyssen) is a vampire hunter and the sea crossing sequence and character of Renfield are absent.

In the film Mina (Melissa Stribling) is married to Arthur Holmwood (Michael Gough). Some of these changes were presumably made with a view to saving money. The film is fairly streamlined at 90 minutes but still serves as a stylish and enjoyable adaptation. There are more faithful versions of Dracula out there but few are as much fun this Hammer version.

Dracula stands out for its atmospheric and visually stunning cinematography. The film artfully uses shadows, light, and colour to create an eerie and Gothic atmosphere, which becomes a character in itself. The makeup and costumes are meticulously crafted, with Dracula's signature cape and hypnotic red eyes elevating his presence as the formidable vampire. Dracula brought a new level of horror and gore to the vampire genre. While the violence may seem relatively mild by today's standards, the film's use of blood, fangs, and disintegrating vampire deaths were highly impactful and groundbreaking at the time.

Dracula propelled Hammer Films into superstardom and firmly established Christopher Lee as the face of Dracula for generations to come. The film's success led to numerous sequels and opened the door for a golden age of British horror cinema. Dracula, like most Hammer pictures, is a very cosy film to watch today in that it always seems comforting and familiar. It is a very important film in the history of Hammer and one of the most purely enjoyable pictures they made. One of the nice things about this version of Dracula too is that it often seems to be playing on my Freeview box whenever I'm flipping around.

A lot of old British horror films can get a bit forgotten but happily that isn't the case with Hammer horror and - especially - Dracula. It's nice to think that new generations are now discovering and enjoying this film.

DRACULA 1972 (1972)

Dracula AD 1972 is a Hammer Horror film directed by Alan Gibson and written by Don Houghton. The film is - as the wonderful title suggests - an attempt by the studio to give their (by then) somewhat tired vampire series some new life and zest with a funky, modern twist, transplanting Dracula (Christopher Lee) from his usual gothic period surroundings into an era when large cravats and bright yellow wallpaper were still perfectly respectable. We begin with a great prologue - which literally drips with Hammer residue - set in 1872 where Van Helsing and Dracula scuffle around on a speeding runaway horse carriage in some spookily dark and foggy forest somewhere.

Dracula ends up impaled on a broken cartwheel and Van Helsing also dies but a mysterious figure is glimpsed collecting some ashes. Flash forward to 1972 and swinging psychedelic Chelsea, conveyed by some gloriously camp seventies music, a jet plane in the sky and random shots of London. Now, 100 years later, Dracula is about to be revived once again by nutty teenage rebel Johnny Alucard (Christopher Neame). Johnny and his gang of fellow teenage hippie tearaways - none of whom look a day under 30 - like to gatecrash stilted posh parties until the occupants have to call the fuzz and everybody makes a run for it.

As much fun as it is ruining the parties of well-heeled folk in a mild comic fashion, Johnny is looking for something new to do for kicks now though and comes up with an interesting suggestion. "A date with the Devil," suggests the little scamp. "A bacchanal with Beelzebub." He somehow (as you do) ends-up resurrecting none other than Dracula ("Master, I did it, I summoned you!") after a black magic ceremony at an old church slated for demolition and, in an extraordinary coincidence for plot purposes, one of Johnny's obstreperous gang just happens to be the buxom young Jessica Van Helsing (Stephanie Beacham), a descendant of Dracula's sworn enemy and granddaughter of occult expert Professor Van Helsing (Peter Cushing). The struggle between Professor Van Helsing and Dracula is about to play out once again - but this time with a backdrop of sideburns and flared trousers.

A fairly ludicrous and often very silly attempt to breathe life into Dracula by Hammer, Dracula AD 1972 is far from the best film to ever come from the legendary studio but most certainly not without its dated charms and unintentional laughs and the presence of Cushing and Lee is - as ever - a big boost to any film. Johnny is of course a descendant of the man who took Dracula's ashes all those years ago and an acolyte of the blood drinking dandy through this family connection, painstakingly passed down through the ages. With Dracula holed-up in the abandoned church, Johnny lures his friends one by one to be victims as Cushing's Professor Van Helsing becomes drawn into these diabolical affairs when Inspector Murray (Michael Coles), puzzled by a rash of bloodless corpses that keep appearing in London, consults him on the occult nature of this developing mystery.

One slight problem with this development is that it often keeps Dracula constricted to the old church and limits Christopher Lee's time onscreen as we follow the capers of the suspiciously old looking and not very hip teenagers. "Okay, okay," says of Johnny's cohorts at the black magic ritual. "But if we do get to summon up the big daddy with the horns and the tail, he gets to bring his own liquor, his own bird and his own pot." It's fun though to see Bond girl Caroline Munro, who later famously chased Roger Moore's Lotus around Sardinia in a helicopter, as Laura Bellows.

The seventies and youth culture trappings might have dated the film from just about the second it came out but these elements are of course all part of the fun now and give Dracula AD 1972 a slight Amicus (Hammer's British rival horror studio at the time and more prone to contemporary settings) air at times, the 'teenagers' also sometimes looking like they've just stepped off the set of a Bless This House spin-off or something where Sid James lives next door to Terry Scott and Robin Askwith probably plays his son. The vague Carry On feeling to the film at times perhaps illustrates why Count Dracula spends the film confined to the Gothic gloom of a church - a far more traditional Hammer environment than a swinging seventies party with pop music and luminous shirts.

Christopher Lee was apparently somewhat unhappy at updating the series and projecting Dracula into modern times and it would probably have seemed a tad jarring to have him, in his famous cape, interacting with the rest of the film to any great degree. Lee is great though as ever and both he and Peter Cushing give far more serious and commanding performances than the film probably deserves. Dracula AD 1972 begins and ends with two great and hugely enjoyable showdowns between Van Helsing and Dracula from the out of control runaway carriage fight in a dark forest to the enjoyable climax here and it always seems iconic when Lee and Cushing face off against one another as these characters.

A lot of actors seem so contemporary you never quite believe in them in a period setting but Peter Cushing was of course always uncannily believable in period capers and plays Van Helsing here in almost an anachronistic way, a descendant who is virtually like having the real Van Helsing. Cushing's greatest ability was to always give a committed and skilfully engaging performance in any film he appeared in, however daft, and he does this to great effect in Dracula AD 1972, carrying much of the picture with his usual quiet charm and flashes of intensity. Cushing's marvellously urbane and cultured voice is also a great pleasure to listen to, especially with dialogue like - "There is evil in the world. There are dark, awful things. Occasionally, we get a glimpse of them. But there are dark corners; horrors almost impossible to imagine, even in our worst nightmares!" Peter Cushing is an actor I could watch in just about anything.

Elsewhere, Christopher Neame does his best to be sinister as Johnny and isn't bad at all - despite coming across sometimes like a poor man's Alex from a Clockwork Orange - with one or two memorable moments. Stephanie Beacham is very well cast though as Dracula's intended revenge victim Jessica, looks great in sacrificial skimpy Hammer film costumes and has a few nice moments with Cushing. "Weird, man. Way out," says Jessica, not entirely escaping the attempts at groovy youth culture dialogue altogether. "I mean, spooks, hobgoblins, black magic. All that sort of stuff." Dracula AD 1972 is absolute nonsense of course but as far as absolute nonsense goes this is great fun at times with the enjoyable seventies trappings and the always welcome presence of the great Peter Cushing and Christopher Lee.

DR PHIBES RISES AGAIN (1972)

Dr Phibes Rises Again, the sequel to The Abominable Dr Phibes, saw Robert Fuest return to direct. This time, Phibes returns and sets off for Egypt to search for a river of eternal life. Darius Biederbeck (Robert Quarry), who has been prolonging his life with an elixir, is also after the same goal and sets off with his team. As you may imagine, with Dr Phibes at large, Biederbeck's team are going to meet some very untimely and elaborate deaths...

Dr Phibes Rises Again is essentially more of the same and - happily - that's exactly what we want. This sequel is not quite on a par with the original but it is a lot of fun. Vincent Price once again rules as the completely mad Phibes and, in his ghoulish white face make-up, gives (if possible) an even more entertainingly bonkers performance than he did in the first film. The deaths are once again amusingly inventive with scorpions, sandblasting, and someone crushed by a giant screw-press. There are some great actors in minor roles here. You get cameos by Peter Cushing, Terry Thomas (playing a different character from the first film) and Beryl Reid. Valli Kemp replaces Virginia North as Vulnavia and her doll like beauty makes her perfect casting.

Caroline Munro returns to play Phibes' late wife Victoria (who Phibes plans to live with for eternity if they can find this famed life preserving river). Look out for a young John Thaw in the cast too. Peter Jeffrey also returns as the not entirely competent policeman Inspector Trout. If anything, this sequel is even crazier than the first film with the art deco designs, Phibes' clockwork band, the bizarre score, and general aura of complete insanity. Despite the camp trappings and preposterous nature of the film it walks a very fine line in never actually falling apart. The actors never play down to the material and the production values are wonderful given the budget.

Robert Quarry (of Count Yorga fame) makes for a solid addition to the cast too, as a sort of rival to Phibes. Biederbeck has stolen the scrolls from Phibes' demolished house and thus taken himself on a path to Egypt. The reputation of this film is slightly confusing because some regard it to be a very inferior cheap sequel. Others (in the minority) like it better than the first film. I'm in the middle myself in that I find Dr Phibes Rises Again to be a perfectly acceptable addition which more or less gives you what you got from the first film. The first film was probably more creative when it comes to the deaths and I'd agree that the original is the better film overall but it isn't as if Dr Phibes Rises Again is a patently inferior sequel. It still has Vincent Price as Phibes, famous guest stars, and plenty of murders! Taken on its own terms this film is still fun!

One flaw in this sequel is that you can see they didn't have the biggest budget in the world when the action moves to Egypt and it all feels very studio bound. The pyramid stuff is very good though. Dr Phibes Rises Again is a fun companion piece to the original film and once again makes the most of Vincent Price and the absolutely insane nature of the world Phibes has created for himself. There were plans for a third Phibes film but sadly these never came to fruition. A Phibes trilogy would have been great but the two films they did make are ample compensation and can be watched over and over again as a fun double bill.

THE FLESH AND THE FIENDS (1960)

The Flesh and the Fiends was directed by John Gilling. The film is based on the case of the famous graverobbers Burke & Hare. There was once a time when digging up fresh corpses from the graveyard and selling them to hospitals and universities was a pretty lucrative business. Strange yes and certainly not legal but also true. Corpses were desperately needed in these institutions in order to teach students about human anatomy and give them something to train with. Cadavers were hard to come by so if you could supply a teaching hospital or place of medical learning with fresh undamaged corpses they were more than happy to pay you good money in return. This led to macabre cases like Burke & Hare and the London Burkers (aka The Bethnal Green Gang).

The most famous exponents of this grisly practice were Burke & Hare. William Burke and William Hare were two men from the north of Ireland who became infamous for their macabre activities in Edinburgh in 1827 and 1828. They came up with what he believed was an ingenious way to make money. Grisly and ghoulish yes but definitely something that had the potential to make them a nice little earner. They took the dead and still fresh body of the deceased boarder to Edinburgh University where anatomy lecturer Professor Robert Knox was more than happy to take it off their hands.

At the time there were strict laws about using corpses for medical research and training medical students. Medical schools and universities could only use the corpses of prisoners, street orphans, or suicides in such research. As a consequence of this there was a chronic shortage of cadavers for medical students and professionals to train and teach with. Hospitals and universities were desperate for dead bodies and willing to pay decent money to get them. Burke and Hare were more than willing to cater to this demand.

Burke & Hare are played by George Rose and Donald

Pleasence in the 1960 film. Peter Cushing plays Professor Robert Knox. Some of the facts of the real case have been changed in the film. The real life women these men consorted with are not in the film and the details of their capture are slightly altered. The general adaptation is pretty good though. It is believed that Burke and Hare killed around sixteen people in all - although the true figure is felt by most to have probably been higher than this. They received between seven and ten pounds for the corpses they sold to the university. When you tally that all up, Burke and Hare collected a tidy sum indeed for their murderous and unusual business activities.

The two men got so greedy and desperate for corpses in the end they even killed a relative of Burke's mistress. Street prostitutes were also among their victims because these were easy targets and not always likely to be missed by anyone or even reported as missing. Burke and Hare found that, when it came to dead bodies for universities and hospitals, demand far outstripped supply and this made them increasingly desperate and ruthless in their attempts to plug the shortfall and increase their profits. It was a simple equation. The more dead bodies they could supply the more money they would make.

Amazingly, Hare was offered immunity to testify against Burke because the prosecution didn't feel they had a huge amount of evidence with which to build a case. This brought protests from the family of victim James Wilson. At the trial, Hare tried to give the impression that he'd had nothing to do with the murders and that William Burke was the driving force behind them. He would say that wouldn't he? William Burke was hanged at Lawnmarket on the 28th of January 1929. The judge ordered that his body should be donated to medical science and publicly dissected. You might say the judge (not unreasonably) considered this punishment to be cosmic karma. Burke's skeleton is now on display at Surgeon's Hall in Edinburgh. William Hare was released in February 1829. He fled to England and essentially vanished.

As for Professor Robert Knox, he was rather disgraced by his association with Burke and Hare and was more or less drummed out of the academic and the medical establishment in Scotland. He never spoke about the case and eventually opened a medical practice far away in London. This film gives Knox a somewhat happier ending than he actually got in real life. The Flesh and the Fiends got a muted reception when it came out but is now considered to be something of a cult film. It is more risque than most other British horror films of the era and has some nudity. Peter Cushing is brilliant and George Rose and Donald Pleasence are also terrific. The sets and costumes are superb and Billie Whitelaw is memorable as a prostitute named Mary. There have been a number of films based on Burke & Hare but this, for my money, is the best of them.

FRENZY (1972)

Frenzy is a 1972 film directed by the legendary Alfred Hitchcock, based on the novel Goodbye Piccadilly, Farewell Leicester Square by Arthur La Bern and adapted for the screen by Anthony Shaffer. The film saw Hitchcock return to Blighty after many years working in the United States and is a suspense thriller set and shot in London, returning to the formula of an ordinary, innocent man in increasingly desperate trouble as he is framed for murders he didn't commit.

In this case, it is down on his luck former RAF pilot Richard Blaney (Jon Finch), now reduced to working as a barman at the Globe Public House and rather too fond of helping himself to the booze which, unsurprisingly, soon leads to the sack. Only a little financial support from his ex-wife, Brenda (Barbara Leigh-Hunt), who runs a dating agency, offers any comfort as Blaney is temporarily forced to sleep in a hostel for the homeless. Meanwhile, London is being rocked by a series of bizarre murders that always involve a woman being strangled by a necktie - which the killer leaves dangling around the neck of the unfortunate victim...

"We haven't had a good juicy series of sex murders since Christie," we overhear someone cheerfully saying in a pub. "And they're so good for the tourist trade. Foreigners somehow expect the squares of London to be fog-wreathed, full of hansom cabs and littered with ripped whores, don't you think?" When Brenda becomes the latest victim of the necktie murderer at her matchmaking office, the innocent Blaney is in very big trouble indeed because he was the last person seen in the vicinity of the offices and was spied being very argumentative and angry with his late ex-wife by her secretary.

He is now the prime suspect for Brenda's murder. "Can you imagine me creeping around London," muses the bewildered Blaney. "Strangling all those women with ties? That's ridiculous...for a start, I only own two." As his situation becomes increasingly desperate, Blaney finds himself relying on his old friend, chirpy cockney Covent Garden fruit trader Bob Rusk (Barry Foster), for help and somewhere to hide.

Frenzy is a highly entertaining twilight return to form by Hitchcock and a film I've always enjoyed a great deal. It's fun to have him back in London and although this is a slightly anachronistic London - more the London of Hitchcock's memory than a real one at times - with some rather overripe cockney accents, the authentic location work (the picture begins with a body being fished out of the Thames) and market bustle always adds a nice atmosphere to the film. The cast is good fun too with Jon Finch veering into so bad he's good territory with a gloriously theatrical turn as the down on his heels Blaney.

Finch has a crisp, loud and plummy thespy voice obviously crafted for the stage but is also a trifle wooden sometimes. The mixture is curiously compelling as he bellows lines like "I distinctly ordered a large Brandy!" to staff in back street pubs as if he was onstage in a production of Richard II or something. "Twenty to bloody one," booms Finch in his posh, over-enunciated way after forgetting to place a bet on a dead cert. "Christ, damn it to hell!" The early scenes, featuring no less than Bernard Cribbens as Felix Forsythe, Blaney's bad-tempered, foul-mouthed, lecherous and thoroughly miserable landlord/boss, are very funny.

There are some really great moments in the film, in particular a fantastic bit where the necktie murderer (who is revealed fairly early on) accidentally leaves important evidence in the hand of a victim he's dumped in some sacks of potatoes. Realising his mistake, he must dive in the back of a moving lorry full of dusty potato sacks and attempt to prize the evidence free from a hand already frozen with rigor mortis by breaking the fingers! It's a wonderful, macabre set-piece full of tension. Another great moment occurs during the (somewhat disturbing) murder of Brenda when Hitchcock pulls the camera away from the scene before things become too grim and takes us on a long, silent tracking shot down the stairs and out into the eventual hustle and noise of the street.

There are some enjoyably showy camera flourishes in Frenzy and this one is quite chilling in effect as we are shown that even if Brenda cried out no one would hear her anyway. Frenzy has several interesting moments where a door or window closes or the camera moves away just as we are about to see or hear something important. The film seems even more risque than Hitchcock's usual fare with some nudity and trademark misogyny and innuendo, but Frenzy also has an almost tongue-in-cheek air at times.

Alec McCowen - who of course played Q in Never Say Never Again if I might be allowed a moment of gratuitous James Bond trivia - is fun too as Chief Inspector Oxford and there are moments of levity and black humour as he discusses the grisly ongoing case with Mrs Oxford (Vivien Merchant) over dinner. "No, discretion is not traditionally the strong suit of the psychopath, dear. Believe me, that's what we're dealing with." Mrs Oxford is undertaking experiments in gourmet cooking and on a French cooking class. She produces various bizarre and inedible dinners for the Chief Inspector, which frequently lead to him having gigantic secret meals of eggs and bacon in his office at the police station. These comic dinner scenes were an addition by screenwriter Anthony Shaffer and deemed superfluous by some critics but personally I've always loved them.

Hitchcock seems to link food to sexual desire as a motif or theme, Chief Inspector Oxford noting that the murderer will kill again - "When his appetite is whetted." McCowen and Merchant are both funny and Mrs Oxford's eccentric and rather meagre interpretations of classic French cuisine are hilarious. McCowen's pained expressions as he warily prods at a plate of pig's trotters or some such with his fork and surreptitiously attempts to dispose of his latest unwanted dinner without his wife seeing him are always amusing. Anna Massey, who I always recall from the classic Amicus anthology film Vault of Horror, also appears as Jane 'Babs' Milligan, a barmaid and girlfriend of Blaney, and Van Der Valk star Barry Foster is good value as the fruit munching Bob Rusk. "Don't forget," says Rusk to Blaney. "Bob's your uncle."

Frenzy lacks Hitchcock's usual gloss, elegant villains and beautiful women (even the hero here is rather threadbare and unlikeable) and has a faintly nasty edge but it is an awful lot of fun too with plenty of twists and turns, audience manipulation, memorable moments, dark humour, in-jokes, and a good cast full of familiar faces. Frenzy was one last return to form for the master of suspense and is well worth watching for anyone who has never seen it before.

By the way, Frenzy was heavily inspired by the Jack the Stripper murders. Hammersmith in London was the scene of a number of grisly murders in 1964 and 1965. The killer became known as Jack the Stripper because the murder victims were all prostitutes and always had their clothes and belongings (including, believe it or not, false teeth) removed. However, despite a huge police operation, the killer was never found and the murders remain a mystery to this day. The puzzling thing about the murders is that none of the victims displayed any evidence of sexual violence. The police detective heading up the search for Jack the Stripper in the 1960s predicted that the case would be as famous as the Jack the Ripper murders. He was obviously completely wrong about that. A lot of people today seem to have barely heard of Jack the Stripper.

The victims were nearly all in their twenties and are believed to have been killed in private before their bodies were dumped in a public place. Chief Superintendent John Du Rose was in charge of the investigation for Scotland Yard and had six-hundred police officers involved in the search for Jack the Stripper. They set up observation posts in a 24 square mile area of London and questioned thousands of potential suspects and yet - remarkably - they never found the killer. So who was Jack the Stripper?

At one point the police seemed to make a breakthrough when analysis of paint particles suggested the victims had been stored at an abandoned factory on the Heron Trading Estate. The police therefore began questioning hundreds of workers on the estate. A man named Mungo Ireland was heavily suspected by the police at one point because he'd worked as a security guard at the estate but Ireland was proven to have been in Scotland when one of the murders took place and was removed from the list of suspects.

One of the prostitute victims of Jack the Stripper had been seen getting into a car with two men before her death but the police could never find these two men or the car in question. This lead though did seem to suggest it wasn't impossible that Jack the Stripper was two men rather than one. Another suspect in the case was an embittered former police detective who lived in the area and had been caught committing burglaries in an attempt to embarrass the police. However, this man could not be linked to the Stripper murders and so was eventually removed from the list of potential suspects.

One of the more outlandish and bizarre theories (which has

even been the basis of a book) is that the killer was the world champion boxer turned actor Freddie Mills. The popular lantern-jawed Freddie Mills was the world light-heavweight boxing champion in 1948 and in retirement had become an actor (he was in two early Carry On films). The notion that Freddie Mills was Jack the Stripper might have started with the gangster Frankie Fraser. The word of Frankie Fraser is not exactly the most empirical evidence.

What gave the Freddie Mills theory traction (which it probably didn't deserve) is that Mills committed suicide not long after the last murder. His suicide is believed to have been a result of financial difficulties due to the failure of his business interests. We should point out too that the police who worked on the Stripper case thought the Freddie Mills theory (which only happened years later) was stupid. They suspect that because Mungo Ireland was also a former boxer some wires might have been crossed somewhere along the line which dragged Freddie Mills (with the aid of some gangster whispers and tittle-tattle) in the game of Stripper suspects bingo.

It is possible (if doubtful) that the real Jack the Stripper might even still be alive today. It is certainly plausible that if Jack the Stripper had been captured the killer would be as famous as British serial killers like Peter Sutcliffe or Dennis Nilsen today. Surprisingly, this killer remains little known - perhaps as a consequence of the fact that he was never caught.

FRIGHTMARE (1974)

Frightmare was directed by Pete Walker and written by Walker and David McGillivray. This is regarded to be the best Pete Walker film and it's hard to argue with that general consensus. Jackie (Deborah Fairfax) is a young woman with big problems. Years ago her parents Dorothy (Sheila Keith) and Edmund (Rupert Davies) were jailed for murder but they've recently been released. That's not even the half of it.

Dorothy was an insatiable cannibal who liked to eat her victims - especially the brains.

Dorothy and Edmund are now living in a country cottage - having been deemed sane by the authorities. Edmund might be sane, in fact he was never mad to start with and always more of an accomplice simply trying to protect his wife than a killer, but the same can't be said of Dorothy. Dorothy is still completely doolally and has started killing people again to satiate her desire for human flesh. As if Jackie didn't have enough problems with her parents, she also has to look after her juvenile delinquent teenage half-sister Debbie (Kim Butcher) - a mouthy little rascal who gets her kicks hanging around with motorcycle ruffians. Can this dreadful state of affairs possibly resolve itself in a happy way? Well, I certainly won't be placing a bet on it that's for sure.

Frightmare is a lot of fun once it gets going. Some of the acting by the younger cast members is a trifle on the wooden side but veterans Rupert Davies and Sheila Keith are great as the parents. Sheila Keith was a Pete Walker regular and this is surely her greatest performance in any of his films. The way Dorothy suddenly spins from nice old lady to complete lunatic during a tarot card reading (this is how she lures victims to the cottage) is fantastic and very creepy. There is some gore and blood in the film but it is often implied more than seen. Dorothy takes (as you do) a drill to the head of a victim at one point but they don't actually show you the drill going in or anything like that. The gore is fun though. There's a pitch forking death, a red hot poker demise, and some grisly practical make-up effects.

The plot has Jackie's psychiatrist boyfriend Graham (Paul Greenwood) digging into the family past in an attempt to help Jackie's obstreperous sister Debbie. That predictably turns out to be a big mistake. What he finds out is rather shocking to say the least. Pete Walker always said his films had no hidden meaning and he was just having fun and trying to stir up some controversy - which is perfectly fine. Frightmare is played straight but has an enjoyably ridiculous plot so it isn't to be taken too seriously. There seems to be a message in Frightmare though that all of this is the fault of the authorities for letting Dorothy go free in the first place. You wouldn't say this gave Frightmare a tough justice anti-rehabilitation message though because Dorothy is no ordinary offender. She's a cannibal! You wouldn't let Jeffrey Dahmer walk out of prison would you?

The weak husband Keith standing by his dotty wife and trying to help cover up her crimes is actually quite realistic because true crime is littered with cases where this sort of thing really happened. The score by Stanley Myers in Frightmare is foreboding and atmospheric and the film is genuinely unsettling and weird - which keeps you on edge. In particular, all the scenes in the dark little country cottage of Dorothy and Edmund are creepy - even when nothing is happening. This is not a cottage that you would want to visit. It is sometimes suggested that Frightmare is like a British version of The Texas Chainsaw Massacre but I don't see too many similarities myslf - despite the fact both revolve around nutty families. The Texas Chainsaw Massacre is a backswoods horror film whereas Frightmare has a lot of city scenes. Dorothy, despite being a cannibal!, is an altogether more urbane villain than anyone in the Sawyer family.

It all builds to an enjoyably chilling conclusion. All bets are off in Frightmare. Literally no one is safe and anything can happen - and that's all part of the fun. Pete Walker definitely had a fascinating little niche of his own in the horror world of the 1970s. His films were a bit rough around the edges but quite stylish in their own way and a lot edgier and more gruesome than the films by Amicus and Hammer. He definitely deserves his own little cloud in British horror film history. Oh, and yes, that is indeed Manuel from Fawlty Towers in the black and white prologue.

FROM BEYOND THE GRAVE (1973)

From Beyond the Grave sadly turned out to be the last of the Amicus anthology films and so marked the end of an era. It was originally titled The Undead and is also known as The Creatures, Tales from Beyond the Grave, and Tales from the Beyond. Some fresh (ahem) blood was brought in for this last anthology, most notably Kevin Connor, who gained his first directing credit here. Connor would go to helm the Amicus ahistorical family adventure caper films The Land That Time Forgot, At the Earth's Core and The People That Time Forgot with Doug McClure in the same decade. The cinematographer Alan Hume (who would later work on both the Star Wars and James Bond franchises) worked well with Connor to give From Beyond the Grave an inventive look.

The framing device in From Beyond the Grave, always a fun component of these films, has Peter Cushing as the enigmatic old owner of Temptations Ltd, a dusty antiques shop (motto: Offers You Cannot Resist) in a small, foggy, anachronistic London backstreet. Cushing, with flat cap, pipe and Northern accent, promises a surprise with every purchase. This is certainly the case for those customers who attempt to cheat him out of some money or half-inch something because this antiques shop is not all that it seems...

The first story is called The Gatecrasher and features David Warner and some extraordinary shirts as Edward Charlton. The somewhat smug Edward makes a big mistake when he swindles Cushing out of some money in Tempations Ltd by pretending he's spotted an antique mirror is a reproduction and attaining this item at a bargain price. Once back in his groovy bachelor pad Edward gradually realises that there is something very strange about this mirror after his friends badger him into holding a seance. In fact, the mirror may contain the spirit of a very nasty character indeed and he's eager to make his presence felt...

The Gatecrasher is an atmospheric and enjoyable segment obviously lifted from similar spooky mirror shenanigans with Googie Withers and Ralph Michael in the 1945 Ealing classic Dead of Night. Weird fog and strange faces appearing in mirrors are always quite creepy and this episode is very enjoyable on the whole as Edward's life is slowly turned upside down. The direction is quite good in this one too with Warner's dodgy flat antics and neighbours wondering what is going on reminding me of that classic Hitchcock film Frenzy a little at times and I love the spooky seance with candlelight and the camera panning past the faces of Edward's friends. There is a nice inventive sequence too where the passage of time is highlighted by a quick montage of the flat and its changing decor and residents. Connor's helming of this segment is very good. Another plus is the presence of David Warner, an actor who is always good value and fully committed to whatever nonsense his agent has put him in. There is a nice final twist also in The Gatecrasher which wraps things up very neatly in suitably spooky fashion.

The second story is called An Act of Kindness and features Ian Bannen as Christopher Lowe, a timid and henpecked husband stuck in a boring office job and married to Mabel, played by Diana Dors in full late career battleaxe mode. Considered a joke at home by Mabel and his son, Lowe befriends threadbare matchbox street vendor and old soldier Jim Underwood (Donald Pleasance) who he passes by on the way to and from work. Lowe comes to enjoy the fact that Jim salutes him and calls him Sir, affording him the respect he never gets at home and, browsing in Temptations Ltd, he tries to buy a Distinguished Service Medal to impress the old soldier. But Cushing's crusty old shop owner wants the certificate to prove Lowe really was with Monty's Eight Army in North Africa as he claims and a decorated war hero so Lowe steals it instead when his back is turned. Impressed by the medal, Jim invites Lowe to his home for some tea where he is soon a regular guest and involved in a relationship with Jim's rather creepy young daughter Emily (Angela Pleasence)...

An Act of Kindness is another good segment featuring a wonderfully uptight performance by Ian Bannen as the frustrated Lowe. His dinner table scenes with Diana Dors are very funny as Dors slams his dinner on the table and generally lets him know she thinks he's a complete idiot. Another plus is of course Donald Pleasence as the deferential old soldier. The thing that makes this segment work, in addition to the enjoyable cast, is the nature of the mystery that unravels. You genuinely have no idea what is going to unfold and why Jim is being so kind and generous to Lowe beyond the fact that he claims to have been in the army. Angela Pleasence is well cast too as Jim's rather odd and mysterious daughter.

The third story lightens the tone slightly and is called The Elemental. It features Ian Carmichael as Reggie Warren, a very posh bowler hat and umbrella businessman. The pompous Reggie makes a big mistake when he assumes Cushing's antiques proprietor is a doddering old fossil who can barely remember his own name and switches some price tags in Temptations Ltd to get an antique snuff box on the cheap. "I hope you enjoy snuffing it," says Cushing. On the way home in the train Reggie is bothered in his compartment by an annoying and rather theatrical woman called Madame Orloff (Margaret Leighton), a professional psychic who tells him he has an 'Elemental' on his shoulder. Reggie of course assumes this woman is mad and goes back to his paper to see what the Test Match score is or something but once home in his unfeasibly gigantic country house with wife Susan (Nyree Dawn Porter) strange things soon start to happen...

The Elemental is often a more frivolous tale than the first two with comic elements but becomes scarier as it goes on and the idea of an invisible demon/ghost sitting on your shoulder is quite a creepy one. Ian Carmichael is fun as the disconcertingly upper-class commuter with a house like an embassy and Margaret Leighton chews up the scenery and spits it out with a ridiculously broad and over the top performance as Madame Orloff that skirts past flamboyant and enters the realm of completely bonkers. Not my favourite segment on offer here but not bad and not without its charms.

The final story is called The Door and stars a suave young Ian Ogilvy as William Seaton. Seaton purchases an ancient ornate door from Temptations Ltd - although we are not quite allowed to see if he ripped off Peter Cushing's spooky Lovejoy or not. Once home Seaton and lovely wife Rosemary (Lesley-Anne Down) find themselves becoming entranced by the door and although they've used it as the entrance to their stationary cupboard, it seems to sometimes open into a very mysterious blue room rather than, you know, pencils and, er, rulers and things.

The Door is decent segment although not that scary and lacking the theatrical blood that occasionally flows in some of the other stories. The design is quite atmospheric though and it looks great at times. This is a fairly decent - if straightforward - ghostly tale and Ogilvy is earnest enough as the haunted door capers escalate. We then go back to Peter Cushing and the antiques shop one more time for an enjoyable end to the film. "The love of money is the root of all evil," he laments sadly.

From Beyond the Grave is a lot of fun overall. The film is well directed and you are kept guessing here and there as to how these tales will resolve themselves. The cast is great, especially Cushing who is wonderful as the bushy eyebrowed shop owner. I particularly like his little looks and comments to himself when some shady looking character takes a browse in his shop. "Naughty, shouldn't have done that." Most of all though,

From Beyond the Grave presents more slightly camp and very British seventies compendium horror antics in the best Amicus tradition. It's a shame really that this was the last anthology hurrah.

GHOST STORIES (2017)

Ghost Stories was written and directed by Andy Nyman and Jeremy Dyson and based on their 2010 stage play of the same name. Nyman plays Phillip Goodman in the film. Goodman is a television presenter who debunks fraudulent psychics and the paranormal. His passion for this work stemmed from his deeply religious father shunning Goodman's sister after she started dating an Asian man. Goodman believes that superstition ruins lives. We see Goodman barging in on a psychic on stage who - while obviously a fraud - is at least giving some comfort to a grieving mother.

One day, Goodman receives a package that turns out to be from Charles Cameron (I can't reveal who plays Cameron because that is a big spoiler). Cameron was a famed paranormal debunker in the seventies and was a big hero to Goodman. Cameron mysteriously vanished and was presumed dead but it seems he is alive and well. Goodman goes to visit Cameron and finds him living in a battered caravan by the sea as a recluse. Cameron tells Goodman that everything he believed was wrong and asks him to find out for himself by investigating three unfathomable paranormal cases. And so, Goodman investigates the three cases - which we also see a depiction of. In that sense, Ghost Stories is a return to the anthology films of yesteryear. The big question though resides in how truthful these cases are. And is Phillip Goodman himself a reliable narrator?

The first case concerns a night watchman named Tony Matthews (Paul Whitehouse). Matthews is a rather broken figure as his daughter suffers from locked-in-syndrome and he feels guilty because he doesn't visit her. Matthews tells Goodman about his frightening encounter with the paranormal. He worked as a night watchman at a disused asylum and had a most terrifying night where he seemed to be plagued by the spirit of a young girl. This first story is quite terrifying at times. It will certainly make you jump if you watch it late at night with headphones. The disused asylum makes an appropriately creepy location for the story and Paul Whitehouse is great too. Whitehouse manages to dispense a few wry quips (mostly aimed at his Eastern European colleague who is in contact on the walkie-talkie) but becomes believably terrified as the night drags on and things become ever stranger.

The second case that Goodman investigates concerns a teenager named Simon Rifkind (Alex Lawther). Rifkind is holed up in his bedroom and a nervous wreck. He tells Goodman about the night he sneaked out in his father's car to attend a party but the car broke down on a lonely road surrounded by woodland. Simon ran something over too. Something 'Devilish' that then seemed to stalk him. This story has a wonderful atmosphere and is very enjoyable. The only thing that might grate somewhat is the over eager and over the top performance of Alex Lawther. You wouldn't really call Lawther subtle here. He's chewing up any and all scenery he can get his teeth into. The only disappointing thing about this story is that it just seems to abruptly fizzle out. I wouldn't have minded this story being longer to be honest.

The third case has Goodman visiting the country home of a city finance hotshot named Mike Piddle (Martin Freeman). Piddle had an encounter with a ghost when his wife was pregnant and he relays this spine tingling tale. This last story is probably the least interesting of the 'backstory segments' but it is very well done all the same and I love Piddle's modernist country house (which appears to be Horton Rounds). Goodman, despite experiencing plenty of strange things in the course of these investigations, is not convinced they are evidence for the paranormal. All can be explained he argues. Matthews was an alcoholic. Rifkind was a confused young man. And so on. However, when he reports back to Cameron, Goodman receives a very big surprise. The film changes course somewhat and becomes vaguely reminiscent of John carpenter's In the Mouth of Madness where reality seems to fall apart at the seams.

The twist at the end revolves around an incident in Goodman's past. I won't spoil this for those who haven't watched the film but it does take Ghost Stories down a slightly unexpected - and more dramatic - path. It gives the film and the character of Goodman more structural depth but if I'm completely honest it wasn't my favourite part of the film and made Ghost Stories a rather depressing experience at times. Still, if you like anthology horror films you should enjoy this on the whole and the cast is very good. It's one of the better British horror films in recent memory and worth seeking out.

GHOSTWATCH (1992)

Ghostwatch is a legendary piece of British television history. Ghostwatch is a drama written by Stephen Volk. The story concerns a live investigation into a haunted house where things go very wrong. Ghostwatch was broadcast on Halloween night in 1992 and has never been repeated. It was deemed too controversial. The blurb in the Radio Times went as follows - 'In this notorious "live" coverage, the most up-to-date television technology seeks to show proof of the supernatural in the first transmission from an alleged haunted house on Halloween night, 1992. Ghosts no longer inhabit stately homes or rattle chains. They live in ordinary council houses like that of Mrs Pamela Early and her two children. For months the family has suffered strange noises, awful smells and bent cutlery, but is hers really the most haunted house in Britain as the tabloids claim? For the first time, BBC TV turns its cameras on the subject of the paranormal, and sends its intrepid reporters to investigate ghoulies, ghosties and things that go bump in the night. Are they real, or just make-believe?'

A large number of viewers that Halloween night were fooled into thinking that they really were watching a live Most Haunted style show. The BBC were deluged with complaints. 'VIEWERS SLAM BBC'S SICK GHOST HOAX!' screamed the tabloids. What seemed to terrify viewers the most was the fact that were taken by surprise. They thought they were safe watching Ghostwatch. They thought this would be cosy and factual. But no one was safe in Ghostwatch - not even the presenters!

Ghostwatch concerns a live BBC television investigation into what is said to be a very haunted house occupied by the Early family on the fringes of London and features several famous television presenters playing themselves - which must have played no small part in fooling the unquantifiable number of viewers who apparently believed it was all real. At the helm of the Ghostwatch broadcast is none other than Michael Parkinson and joining him to man the telephone lines and read out ghostly sightings and musings from the viewing public is the late Mike Smith. "No creaking gates," says Parky, setting the scene. "No gothic towers, no shuttered windows. Yet for the past ten months this house has been the focus of an astonishing barrage of supernatural activity."

They are joined in the studio by psychic researcher Dr Lin Pascoe (Gillian Bevan) and out on presenting duties at the haunted house and location are children's television presenter Sarah Greene and Craig Charles of Red Dwarf fame. Pam Early (Brid Brennan) and her children Suzanne (Michelle Wesson) and Kim (Cherise Wesson) have experienced various strange and troubling supernatural phenomena in the house which seems to stem from the rather disturbing presence of a ghost known as 'Pipes' because of the clanging metallic noises that herald his arrival, the sound reminiscent of a rattling clapped-out central heating system.

"Well, maybe they're both involved," offers Dr Pascoe in the television studio. "I mean, maybe it's like a tandem effect. Kim's creating the energy and Suzanne's directing the violence in on herself." All seems relatively serene as the investigation begins at the house and the dubious Parky soon adopts a sceptical attitude back in the safety of the studio. But is this the calm before the storm?

This is in many ways part of a classic trilogy of ghostly British television classics alongside Whistle and I'll Come to You and The Stone Tape and an inventive and genuinely creepy piece of Halloween mischief from the BBC heavily inspired by the work of Nigel Kneale. Ghostwatch is a wonderfully devious film that seems disarmingly benign for a while and rather like watching an episode of Crimewatch or something - a programme which it vaguely seems to be a satire of in a postmodern fashion. Interestingly, Ghostwatch must predate Most Haunted by a good ten years or so and also touches on the manipulation of reality television and audiences - which places it somewhat ahead of its time as reality television was far less ubiquitous around this period and not the staple of the schedules that it is today.

Ghostwatch goes to great lengths to make everything seem authentic and mimic a real outside broadcast with the famous presenters playing themselves, infrared and close circuit cameras, and Mike Smith reading out viewers messages and calls about things they may have spotted during the broadcast as if it's all completely live. While this is all done very well I'm a little surprised that some people seemed to think it was genuine. After a while it becomes apparent that people are acting rather behaving in a completely natural manner but it doesn't really matter now I suppose as we know this was simply a fiendish and enjoyable sort of semi-hoax.

The haunting under investigation in Ghostwatch gradually becomes more creepy and interesting as the drama unfolds and we duly see some film of the ghostly activity which leads to a number of calls from 'viewers' who believe they may have seen a shadowy figure in one of the bedrooms. Use of CCTV footage is nicely incorporated into the film and effectively eerie and ambiguous at times. Michael Parkinson maintains a scoffing attitude in the studio though and one of the real strengths of Ghostwatch I think is that it's hard to believe that anything bad or scary can ever really happen with the Parkinson presiding over matters and children's television favourite Sarah Greene in the haunted house investigating.

The ordinary suburban setting and presence of these cosy family favourites makes Ghostwatch more unsettling and effective. Craig Charles - who is perhaps just a tad ripe in his own performance on occasion and the one person who threatens to give the game away - is deployed for one fake jump to sort of pull the rug under the audience and make them believe nothing ghostly is really going on. It's very clever stuff on the whole and all builds to a wonderfully weird climax that is pure Nigel Kneale.

The ghost known as 'Pipes' starts to play a larger role in the narrative as we learn more about him and this ups the creepiness factor to Ghostwatch and is good fun. Pipes, the old rascal, takes his name from the banging sound that he causes and the younger daughter explains that he's absolutely hideous in appearance and lives in a cupboard under the stairs - which in my view would surely make him qualify for some sort of discount in his rent. She even draws a picture of this pesky ghost and before long the elder daughter is speaking in a horrible guttural voice as Craig Charles investigates the local area and discovers all manner of strange things have been happening in the neighbourhood.

As events in the house become stranger and stranger, Parky tells the viewers that they'll be staying on air and the next programme will be delayed. The 'viewers' themselves, far from crestfallen at the temporary postponement of the next show, were now bombarding the studio with calls saying they saw a strange figure again as the grisly origins of the haunting begin to fall into place. Even though we now know it wasn't real, Ghostwatch is still far scarier than any episode of Most Haunted could ever hope to be and a classic piece of spine chilling mischief. The self referential construction is a lot of fun as events become ever weirder. It's just a shame that - perhaps because of the rumpus that followed - Halloween night on British television has probably never been quite the same ever since.

HELLRAISER (1987)

Hellraiser was written and directed by Clive Barker and based on Barker's 1986 novella The Hellbound Heart. In this film an ordinary house hides a dark secret. A man named Frank (Sean Chapman) is secretly lurking the attic. He solved a puzzle box called the Lament Configuration and opened a doorway to another dimension - which looked an awful lot like Hell. Demonic figures known as Cenobites emerged and killed Frank in a most grisly fashion. Or did they?

Frank is resurrected by blood but in order to fully repair his body he's going to need an awful lot more. Frank's brother Larry (Andrew Robinson) moves into the house with his wife Julia (Clare Higgins). Unknown to Larry, Julia once had an affair with Frank and she is willing to facilitate his desperate need for blood. Frank's daughter Kirsty (Ashley Laurence), who has a difficult relationship with Julia, may prove to be the biggest obstacle when it comes to Frank and Julia's diabolical plans.

Hellraiser was made in England but the studio New Line later decided they wanted it to be set in America. To this end, they dubbed some American accents into the film and pretended it was set in America - which it clearly isn't. Clive Barker made light of this on the audio commentary. As he notes, you can clearly see a very British train go past at one point! When New line dubbed American accents into Hellraiser to make it seem like it was set in America, they even planned at one point to have an actor dub over Doug Bradley as Pinhead! Thankfully, good sense prevailed in the end and Bradley's performance was left intact. It would have been a travesty if Bradley was dubbed because his version of Pinhead is one of the greatest horror villains of all time.

Doug Bradley's version of Pinhead is a patient and rather mannered sort of monster as far as horror villains go. Jason Vorhees and Michael Myers never speak while Freddy Krueger is something of an evil jester. Leatherface makes strange noises but that's about it. The articulate Pinhead was different though in that while he was completely evil and literally the last person you'd ever want to meet (not unless you want to be ripped apart by chains and live in Hell for all eternity that is), he would actually engage in intelligent conversation with some of his victims before he unleashed dreadful Cenobite fury down upon them.

It might be stretching things to say that Pinhead would be perfectly at home dispensing bon mots at a summer garden party over cucumber sandwiches but he was a much more civilised and conversational monster than many of his 80s horror counterparts. In a way, this misleading sense of urbane civility made Pinhead more scary than mute knife wielding monsters or masked maniacs with chainsaws. Pinhead will drag you to Hell and snap your bones but he'll do it in a measured sort of fashion and take the time to talk to you. You could say that Pinhead likes to chew his food properly before he digests it. On the set of Hellraiser, Clive Barker instructed Doug Bradley to be very minimal in his movements because Pinhead was not the type of person who needed to do anything to be threatening.

Hellraiser was made in the last era of practical effects before CGI gradually took over. The resurrection of Frank from his skeletal state remains an incredible sequence. The Cenobites are fantastic creations and the fog smoked hell dimension of spooky decayed corridors they inhabit are well designed. The opening sequence where Frank experiments with the puzzle box and summons the Cenobites is fantastic. There's a great cast in this film too with Andrew Robinson as the doomed Larry and Claire Higgins as Julia - one of the most memorable human monsters in any horror film. Ashley Laurence is also appealing and likeable as the young heroine Kirsty.

Hellraiser is a true horror classic and a film that rewards repeat viewings. For better or for worse, Hellraiser became a franchise which later spawned some dreadful straight to DVD entries. I would though recommend Hellbound: Hellraiser II - which is a fairly solid sequel. Trivia -the makers of Hellraiser were very annoyed when the famous British film critic Barry Norman (who had a weekly film review show on the BBC) trashed the movie. They were especially irritated because it was for all and intents and purposes a British film industry movie and they felt as if Norman should be more supportive. As a consequence of this they invited Norman to visit the set of Hellraiser II. During his visit Barry Norman confessed to them that he just didn't like horror movies - which would explain why he'd hated Hellraiser. Norman conceded to them though that films should be judged on their individual merit - regardless of what genre they fell into.

HORROR EXPRESS (1972)

Horror Express is a 1972 British-Spanish horror film directed by Eugenio Martín. This film has a great cast with Christopher Lee, Peter Cushing, and Telly Savalas. The first time I ever watched this film I was struck by how much the plot reminded me of John Carpenter's The Thing - only set on a train rather than in some ice glazed wilderness. It was only later that I found out that Horror Express was based on John W. Campbell's 1938 novella Who Goes There? - which was the basis for The Thing from Another World and Carpenter's classic remake. As you can imagine, I felt a bit daft about that.

Anyway, what is the plot of Horror Express? It is 1906 and an anthropologist named Sir Alexander Saxton (Christopher Lee) has discovered a prehistoric creature frozen in the Siberian wilderness. Saxton is understandably eager to keep this discovery secret. As the creature is transported on the Trans-Siberian Express, it comes back to life and starts killing the passengers on board. The creature can absorb the memories, skills, and the appearance of its victims. Also on the train is Dr Wells (Peter Cushing), Saxton's friendly rival from the Geological Society.

Horror Express is a very enjoyable romp which moves at a fast clip and has an attractive colourful look. The horror intrigue is effectively spooky and there is plenty of incident and action too - not least when Telly Savalas turns up as the no nonsense Captain Kazan and delivers an enjoyably over the top performance as he starts throwing his weight around and threatening everyone in over the top fashion. Telly seems to be enjoying himself playing this brash macho character and part of the fun comes from knowing that Kazan and his men are wading out of their depth without even knowing it. They are meddling, to use a horror cliche, with forces they don't understand.

Christopher Lee and Peter Cushing deliver great performances as these two very English fish out of water characters trapped on this crazy train and the film is consistently inventive and entertaining - making its constrictive location a strength rather than a weakness. The train becomes like an extra character in the film as it hurtles through the snow. Horror Express is basically a fun B-picture that makes the most out of its premise and cast and delivers a lot of fun and plenty of creepy horror. The film has some great lines too thanks to the witty script.

The film's strength lies in its ability to keep viewers guessing throughout. As the bodies pile up and the tension rises, questions concerning the nature of the creature and its terrifying abilities surface. While early on, Horror Express appears to be a traditional monster movie, it swiftly evolves into a gripping whodunit murder mystery with supernatural elements thrown in for good measure. The practical effects in Horror Express, especially considering the film's era, are commendable. The creature design itself is impressive, showcasing meticulous attention to detail that adds an extra layer of horror to the narrative.

Additionally, the film's practical effects serve to heighten the tension and contribute to several genuinely terrifying moments. Horror Express is a beloved entry in the horror genre and a must-watch for fans of vintage horror films. Its combination of talented actors, atmospheric setting, and suspenseful storytelling make it an enjoyable and memorable viewing experience. Horror Express is great fun and one of the most purely enjoyable British (and Spanish!) horror films from this era. If you've ever wondered what The Thing would look like if it was a period piece set on a train, well, Horror Express will satisfy that curiosity.

THE HOUND OF THE BASKERVILLES (1959)

There have been countless versions of Sir Arthur Conan Doyle's timeless The Hound of the Baskervilles made for cinema and television over the years but one of my own personal favourites is this 1959 adaption by Hammer Studios, an enjoyably melodramatic and Gothic spin on the famous tale starring the great Peter Cushing as Sherlock Holmes. Holmes purists might find a few elements to nitpick over but the film is wonderfully rich in Hammer residue and great fun on the whole. It begins with an unmistakably Hammer-esque prologue set back in the 1600s where the wicked aristocrat Sir Hugo Baskerville (David Oxley) kidnaps a local servant wench for his pleasure and hunts her down ("Let loose the pack!") on the moors when she escapes and makes a run for it.

At an old mist shrouded abandoned ruined abbey near Baskerville Hall he murders the unfortunate girl but is then almost immediately killed himself by what appears to be a giant spectral hound - thus starting the terrifying legend of the Hound of the Baskervilles. Since then every male Baskerville heir has died in strange circumstances when venturing too close to the moors alone, an apparent victim of an ancient curse on the family.

When the latest heir to Baskerville dies in creepy circumstances at the remains of the abbey, family friend Dr

Mortimer (Francis De Wolff) travels to London to consult the legendary detective Sherlock Holmes (Peter Cushing) and his assistant Dr Watson (Andre Morell) and ask them to examine this very spooky and troubling mystery. "Do you imagine that I can prevent the Powers of Darkness?" muses Cushing in his delightfully urbane voice as Holmes. Holmes duly agrees to look into matters but explains that he has urgent business to attend to elsewhere for the time being and places Watson in charge of the case, requesting that he goes to stay at Baskerville Hall to keep an eye on the new owner, Sir Henry (Christopher Lee)...

Hammer do a fine job with Conan Doyle's most famous story and reel you in right from the start with the atmospheric prologue which broadens the film out a little and gives it a more cinematic gloss. Once back in the 'present' day and inside the cosy firelit rooms of 10 Baker Street, it is apparent fairly quickly that Peter Cushing makes a wonderful Sherlock Holmes. He's energetic, eccentric, brilliant, kind, aloof and always great fun to be with as he pits his considerable intellect against the uncanny mystery of the Baskerville curse.

Cushing doesn't have the rangy physical presence of Basil Rathbone or the angst of Jeremy Brett but he gives a very commanding performance nonetheless that makes you wish Hammer had tackled a few more Holmes adventures with him, something which they had apparently planned to do but never got around to. Cushing did play Holmes again on television later but the budgets and sets were a far cry from the glossy and atmospheric production on offer here from Hammer and, sadly, only a handful of episodes remain because in those days the BBC used to 'wipe' tapes to record over them again. If only they had known there would be entire television stations devoted to old programmes in the future!

"Superficial," dismisses Cushing's Holmes here after a brilliant piece of deduction on his part. "There is nothing remarkable about using one's eyes." Cushing's crisp delivery of these Sherlockian lines is always fun. The thing I love about Peter

Cushing is that he's always absolutely committed to whatever part he's playing and brings a sense of authenticity, be it Sherlock Holmes in Victorian London, battling kung fu vampires in the Far East or, er, fending off a giant octopus with Doug McClure. Another plus in Hammer's version of The Hound of the Baskervilles I think is Andre Morell as Watson. The Basil Rathbone films, as enjoyable as they are, tended to use Watson for comic relief and depicted him as a buffoonish old dodderer. Morell plays it straight and his brave, dependable and decent Watson - who lest we forget is supposed to be a former military man - feels closer to the Watson of the books.

Hammer play slightly fast and loose with the novel at times, adding a few distinct theatrical horror caper elements such as the mist shrouded prologue, a missing tarantula and sacrificial rites. They do an excellent job though in terms of atmosphere and this is a wonderful film to watch late at night with the large, creaky antique rooms of Baskerville Hall casting long shadows and strange lights on the damp, foggy moors at night. One thing that can become a problem with this oft-adapted tale is of course the fact that Holmes is offscreen for the middle portion of the story. Here though, Morell manages to carry the picture along fairly well as Watson settles into Baskerville Hall and meets the various local characters who may or may not be red herrings. The cast is enjoyable on the whole with Miles Malleson hamming it up as the eccentric and forgetful Bishop Frankland ("Bishop of the Upper Isles... for what they're worth") and Ewen Solon as neighbour Stapleton with Marla Landi as his exotic daughter Cecile. The film also plays up the class distinctions of the era more than other interpretations. "When you're poor, no one wants to know you," laments a key character.

The middle section of the film is pleasantly mysterious with Hammer deploying their vast experience in creating spooky landscapes and sets with dim lights coming from isolated old houses. The escaped convict on the moor strand to the story is nicely done here too and the film has some great moments when Watson detects strange flickerings outside in the dead of night. Once Cushing re-enters the film though it really picks up the pace and builds to an entertaining final act. Although the film isn't completely faithful to the book, Cushing himself has obviously gone to great lengths to delve into the literary roots of the character and his Holmes is admirably enigmatic at times, always two or three steps ahead of everybody else but keeping his cards close to his chest.

By the end of the film you are convinced that this is a brilliant man and that Cushing IS Sherlock Holmes. One thing I really like about Cushing's Holmes is that he's very energetic, almost athletic, as he rushes around the desolate countryside from ruined buildings to abandoned mines, eager to corroborate his theories and suspicions. I don't think Conan Doyle's Holmes ever actually said "elementary, my dear Watson" but it's absolutely fantastic when Cushing says it here just for the polished and wonderful way he pronounces the word "elementary". Cushing's palpable enthusiasm is infectious and gives the film a big boost.

Christopher Lee is also excellent in the film as Sir Henry. Lee was apparently tiring of playing the same roles all the time and seems to enjoy himself as a more vulnerable and slightly timid character up to his neck in a mystery he doesn't understand. He affects great terror in a memorable scene involving in a tarantula. It's always a great pleasure to be in the company of actors like Christopher Lee and Peter Cushing for 90 minutes or so and consequently The Hound of the Baskervilles is highly enjoyable. The film has a wonderful closing image of Holmes and Watson together with a final line that never fails to make me smile. Hammer's spin on The Hound of the Baskervilles is very good on the whole with two of my favourite actors of all time and a wonderfully foggy and mysterious atmosphere. This is well worth a look if you've never seen it before, especially if you are a fan of Sherlock Holmes.

THE INNOCENTS (1961)

The Innocents was directed by Jack Clayton. The film is based on the 1898 novella The Turn of the Screw by Henry James. The adaptation for the screen included contributions by John Mortimer and Truman Capote. The film tells the story of a governess named Miss Giddens (Deborah Kerr) who is hired by a wealthy man (Michael Redgrave) to take care of two orphaned children at a remote English country estate. Miss Giddens begins to suspect that the children, Flora (Pamela Franklin) and Miles (Martin Stephens), are possessed by malevolent spirits or ghosts that only she can see. As she investigates the paranormal occurrences, she slowly descends into madness, questioning her own sanity and the reality of the situation.

The film masterfully creates a haunting atmosphere, with Gothic imagery and eerie music, effectively building tension throughout. It explores themes of innocence, corruption, and sexual repression. Deborah Kerr delivers a superb performance as Miss Giddens, capturing her vulnerability, fear, and determination to protect the children. The child actors, Martin Stephens and Pamela Franklin, also give convincing performances as the mysterious and sometimes unsettling Flora and Miles. I should mention too that Megs Jenkins is great as Mrs Grose and you also get Jason King himself Peter Wyngarde as Peter Quint.

The Innocents wa praised for its atmospheric cinematography and its ability to keep audiences guessing whether the supernatural events are real or merely a product of Miss Giddens' imagination. It has been recognised as a classic within the horror genre and has influenced many subsequent films (the Nicole Kidman film the Others certainly owes something to The Innocents). The innocents is considered one of the most chilling and thought-provoking horror films of the 1960s.

The eerie and haunting sound design, along with Georges Auric's chilling score, contribute immensely to the film's atmospheric impact. The sparing use of music, coupled with the utilisation of ambient sounds, heightens the tension and enhances the eerie ambiance. The combination of unsettling auditory cues and silence builds an ever-present sense of impending doom, never allowing the viewer to fully relax. Jack Clayton's masterful direction, coupled with the stunning visuals and impeccable sound design, creates an unforgettable cinematic experience. This psychological thriller flawlessly unravels a chilling tale of ghostly encounters, psychological torment, and the frailty of the human psyche.

The Innocents was shot at Shepperton but Sheffield Park and Garden was used for the outdoor manor scenes. Sheffield Park and Garden is an informal landscape garden five miles east of Haywards Heath, in East Sussex. It was originally laid out in the 18th century by Capability Brown, and further developed as a woodland garden in the early 20th century.

The outdoor location work in the film is very charming. This film also works wonderfully in black and white. You can't quite imagine The Innocents as a colour film - it just wouldn't be the same. This film is sometimes compared to The Haunting - another classic black and white chiller which came out around the same time. The films do have some similarities in that they revolve around a troubled central heroine and work on the premise that what we imagine is often scarier than what we can see.

The Innocents has a fantastic sense of atmosphere and is a very classy chiller. The film is well cast and brilliantly directed. Jack Clayton went out of his way to make this film look and feel different from the Hammer pictures - not because the Hammer pictures aren't great but because he wanted The Innocents to be its own thing. You could sort of describe The Innocents as a prestige horror film in that it is an exceptionally well made drama which just happens to be a mystery with supernatural themes.

KILL LIST (2011)

Kill List was directed by Ben Wheatley and co-written and co-edited with Amy Jump. What would happen if one of those Rise of the Footsoldier crime films had a baby with The Wicker Man? Well, the end result might turn out something like Kill List. Jay (Neil Maskell) is a former soldier turned hitman who lives with his wife Shel (MyAnna Buring) and son Sam (Harry Simpson). Jay, we learn, was deeply affected by something that happened on a job in Kiev. His marriage is under strain because he hasn't worked for a while and money is tight. One evening his old army friend and fellow hitman Gal (Michael Smiley) comes for dinner with his new girlfriend Fiona (Emma Fryer). Gal has a proposition for Jay. A job that will involve Jay and Gal killing three people - a priest, 'librarian', and politician. Jay, in need of the money, agrees to take the job. However, this job turns out to be increasingly strange and mysterious - right from the start too because the employer insists on the contract being signed in blood.

Kill List is sort of unique in that it begins as a family drama, then becomes a crime film about hitmen, then takes a sharp turn into folk horror. It manages to juggle all these different genres fairly well though and once you get through the early scenes (which involve a lot of domestic bickering and shouting - this does tend to grate a bit) the film then pulls you in and becomes very compelling. The strange group that hires Jay and Gal is never really explained, which might frustrate some viewers, but this does allow for more mystery as you just have to fill in some of the blanks for yourself. It's quite an interesting concept to have a crime film suddenly plunge into horror - although the clues that this is a horror film are laced in from fairly on.

Neil Maskell is decent enough in the lead and his background in violent British geezer films like Rise of the Footsoldier and The Football Factory means he is perfectly at home in the role of a sarky working-class hitman. Michael Smiley is good casting as Gal and supplies some levity in a film that gets quite grim at times. These two actors have a believable chemistry so you buy the concept that these are old friends who have been on these sorts of jobs together before. The interesting thing about this film is that it seems eager to evade any distinct category. Some of the early scenes could pass for a kitchen sink drama but it quickly spins away from this.

The crime stuff in the middle is absorbing enough - although some of the violence is a bit much at times. I'm talking about the hammer scene in particular. Ben Wheatley said he included this moment of horrific violence because he wanted to put the audience on edge and feel like the film was capable of doing anything. You could argue that Kill List only becomes a horror film in its last act - although there are weird little details throughout which amp up the increasingly sinister tone. Kill List is one of those films that is interesting to watch again to see how many little clues and indicators you missed early on.

One example of the weird little details comes when Jay's hand becomes infected after he has to shed blood for the contract signing. However, his usual doctor is replaced by someone new - who seems to offer not medical advice but vague philosophy instead. It is pretty clear that the mysterious group who hired Jay to do these killings have replaced his doctor. This group seem to have tentacles everywhere.

The lurch that Kill List takes into horror in the last act is very gripping as Jay and Gal stumble across these weird cultists in the woods who seem to be staging a human sacrifice. The two hitmen are soon running for their lives and seemingly trapped in a dark claustrophobic tunnel. Kill List builds to a very strange ending which is designed to be as shocking as possible. It is a shocking ending but I can't say I was completely surprised by it. The film seemed to be funnelling us towards some shocking twist and there was always a very obvious place to go with this considering that Jay kills people for a living. Nonetheless though you definitely won't forget this ending after you've seen the film.

The motivation of the cultists in the film is never explained so we are left to make of the ending what we want. Wheatley dislikes too much exposition and story and prefers a more visual and enigmatic form of storytelling - which is fine. Kill List is a strange film to be sure, jumbling up as it does all these different elements, but it is well directed and very compelling once it gets going. The horror elements work very well and the last act becomes very gripping.

THE LEGEND OF HELL HOUSE (1973)

The Legend of Hell House is a 1973 British horror film directed by John Hough and adapted by Richard Matheson from his own novel. The film is much in the vein of The Haunting and House on Haunted Hill and revolves around an investigation into a remote and spooky fog-shrouded country mansion. The plot has the wealthy but dying Rudolph Deutsch (Roland Culver) setting a challenge for physicist and parapsychology expert Dr Lionel Barrett (Clive Revill). Deutsch has a large bet of £100,000 with Barrett and will pay out if the physicist can prove or disprove life after death. He challenges Barrett to stay in an abandoned haunted mansion for a week to investigate and see if he can detect anything and the house he chooses is the most haunted house in the world - The Belasco House, better known as Hell House and described as "The Mount Everest of haunted houses!"

Barrett is joined for his stay in Hell House by his wife Ann (Gayle Hunnicutt), a medium called Florence Tanner (Pamela Franklin) who is eager to make contact with any spirits in the mansion, and psychic medium Benjamin Fischer (Roddy McDowall) - who was the only survivor of a previous investigation into the house twenty years before. "I was the only one to make it out of here alive and sane in 1953 and I will be the only one to make it out of here alive and sane this time!"

declares our bespectacled optimist. Yes, thanks for the tremendous confidence booster there Benjamin.

Imagine a slightly camper, colour, British version of The Haunting that isn't as good or stylish and you aren't far off describing The Legend of Hell House which, while not a classic, is a solid enough entry in the haunted house stakes and a decent film in its own right despite reminding you of various other ghostly cinematic ventures. In its favour is a brooding atmosphere, some impressive sets and a spooky electronic score by Delia Derbyshire and Brian Hodgson. Although the film seems to have been slightly forgotten these days it does show signs of a bit of money and ambition at times, at least in comparison to some of the more cheapo British horror films of the seventies. It can never quite seem to completely shake off its somewhat derivative qualities but it is well made and decent fun.

The opening sequence of the characters arriving at Hell House and peering through the iron gates and mist towards spires and towers is nicely done and immediately sets up an eerie aura of dread, continued when the group are greeted upon their arrival inside by a rather creepy gramophone recording by a notorious previous owner of the house - the sadistic Emeric Belasco. "Welcome to my house. I'm delighted you could come. I'm certain you will find your stay here most illuminating. Think of me as your unseen servant, and believe that during your stay here I shall be with you in spirit. May you find the answer that you seek. It is here, I promise you."

Belasco vanished into thin air many years ago after infecting the house with evil through his obstreperous and unusual lifestyle choices. "Drug addiction, alcoholism, sadism, bestiality, mutilation, murder, vampirism, necrophilia, cannibalism, not to mention a gamut of sexual goodies. Shall I go on?" says Fischer when asked to supply a capsule biography of the old rascal. Just to clarify, Belasco was a divisive character and he never quite managed to make it onto This Is Your Life. It appears, after a seance, that the spirit of Daniel

Belasco, son of Emeric, roams the house and the younger Belasco soon begins to make life difficult for the temporary new occupants of Hell House, attempting to bump off Dr Barrett by various means and making all manner of strange things happen to Miss Tanner. It's probably safe to say that Derek Acorah and Yvette Fielding wouldn't have lasted ten minutes in this house.

Revill's parapsychology expert Lionel Barrett is the dedicated and logical man of science although his neglect of his wife is soon picked up on by the house, the ghostly presence turning Anne into a rampant nymphomaniac who disrobes at the drop of a hat and keeps trying to seduce Roddy McDowall's geeky psychic Benjamin Fischer. Fischer is still traumatized by his last visit to Hell House and has erected a physic wall around himself for protection, as you do. He doesn't want to be there at first but slowly builds up an anger against the house and becomes more determined to get to the bottom of the haunting. Roddy McDowell is suitably aloof and eccentric throughout The Legend of Hell House and his earnest (if slightly melodramatic) performance is a boost to the film.

McDowell is a tad broader than the other actors in the film, presumably because unlike them he learned his craft in the United States, but he's good value as ever. I'm a big fan of McDowell through things like the Planet of the Apes series, the Adam West Batman series (where he played Bookworm) and the classic Twilight Zone episode People Are Alike All Over and I always enjoy the fact that he gave everything for each film or television series he was in, however daft it was. I always find it quite charming too that McDowell was evacuated to the United States with his family during the Blitz as a child and made his life and career there but never completely lost his pleasantly anachronistic English accent.

Although the inanimate objects taking on a ghostly life of their own, creaky noises and swinging chandelier capers are all familiar from other films in the same (no pun intended!) spirit, this is certainly very competently done with unusual camera angles and some tight editing - plus the enjoyably menacing electronic soundtrack. The director Jon Hough is probably best known for the Hammer film Twins of Evil and does a solid job here. The Legend of Hell House is more of a psychological horror where we never really see ghosts or monsters and what we imagine is always much scarier than what we see. I also quite like the external shots of the house (filmed at Wykehurst Park, East Sussex) in the film which are always suitably foggy and atmospheric.

There is a Nigel Kneale quality to The Legend of Hell House with the battle between science and the supernatural and this element is further deployed - and the film duly becomes slightly dafter and more vaguely sci-fi - when Barrett unveils a 'reverser' machine, a big box like something out of a Gerry Anderson television series, which he believes will drain the house of its psychic energy and send the spirit of Belasco's dead son, Daniel, away. The house is a gigantic battery "full of mindless, directionless power" and Dr Barrett believes his machine will suck the energy out and set the house free from the evil that lurks there. It's a bit silly but I rather enjoyed this Ghostbusters meets Space 1999 element thrown into the latter half of the film. You can probably guess what is going to happen but it's good fun anyway.

It's enjoyable to see the controlled Barrett attempt to battle these dark forces - though with dire warnings from Fischer. "Belasco doesn't like it, his people don't like it, and they will fight back and they will kill you. So listen to me. You just leave that damn machine alone and you spend the rest of the week resting, doing nothing. When Sunday comes, you tell old Deutsch anything he wants to hear and bank the money. If you try anything else, you will be a dead man, with a dead wife at your side!" Barrett believes that the mediums are conducting the electrical energy in the house and seems largely unconcerned with all the doom laden warnings. One nice touch in the film is having the two mediums, Fischer and Miss Tanner, disagree on the nature of the haunting and which course of action to take.

Flaws in The Legend of Hell House? Clive Revill is perhaps a tad wooden and unmemorable as Dr Barrett - a more urbane choice of actor might have worked better, like that old smoothie Peter Bowles for instance who turns up as Culver's snobby lawyer early in the film. Pamela Franklin is good though as Miss Tanner, who becomes like a magnet for the energy in the house and is also attacked by a possessed cat! Michael Gough (best known now for being Alfred in the Tim Burton Batman films) also makes a cameo near the end although the resolution of the film is not its biggest card and is fairly ludicrous when you actually think about it. I do find the final part of this film highly amusing but I'm not entirely sure that was the intention. It's probably best to say the ending is really rather flawed and eccentric although not entirely devoid of fun.

You could probably say that if the film lacks anything it's a bit of wit and charm at times. While the ghostly goings on are well handled and the film cultivates an enjoyably spectral atmosphere, it doesn't have the polish and slickness of something like The Haunting and is certainly less scary than that black and white classic. On the whole though, although a tad daft and derivative in places, I quite like The Legend of Hell House despite its evident flaws. A fun film to watch late at night if you are in the right mood and one that probably deserves to be slightly better known than it is now.

THE LEGEND OF THE GOLDEN 7 VAMPIRES (1974)

The Legend of the 7 Golden Vampires is a 1974 Hammer film written by Don Houghton and directed by Roy Ward Baker. This was the last Dracula outing they made and is genuinely one of the most bonkers films in cinematic history. The film is a fusion of vampire horror and kung fu capers designed to take advantage of (then) current trends and was a co-production between Hammer and Hong Kong's Shaw Brothers Studios.

The story begins in 1804 with Chinese warlord Kah (Shen Chan) awakening Dracula (John Forbes-Robertson) in his Romanian castle. Transylvania looks suspiciously more like Hong Kong than Romania but anyway.

"Who dares to disturb the sanctity of Dracula?" he is warned after Dracula rises from his long slumber and I know I'm a little grouchy too in the morning if I haven't had at least 200 years. Kah is a "priest" for the 7 Golden Vampires of China and wants Dracula to resurrect them to instill some good old-fashioned fear in the population again. Dracula thanks him for this most interesting suggestion and then promptly kills him and assumes his identity before heading for China.

We then flash forward to 1904. Professor Lawrence Van Helsing (the legendary Peter Cushing) is in China with his foppish son Leyland (Robin Stewart) lecturing on philosophy, parapsychology and, of course, vampires. Legend has it there is one village in particular riddled with the blood sucking scamps according to Van Helsing. After the lecture he is approached by young Hsi Ching (David Chiang) who tells him the legend is real and asks him to lead an expedition to this dreaded village to destroy the vampires.

Chiang's six brothers and one sister are all martial arts experts and he assures Van Helsing they will protect him. Van Helsing is concerned this will all cost a lot of money but - luckily - Scandinavian Bo Derek lookalike and adventuress Vanessa Buren (Julie Ege) just happens to be on hand to supply the funding. So Professor Van Helsing, Leyland, Vanessa and the karate chopping siblings set off on their perilous quest where Dracula - now disguised as a Chinese warlord lest we forget - awaits with the Golden vampires and an army of the undead.

"In Europe the vampire walks in dread of the crucifix," says the professor. "Here it will be the image of the Lord Buddha." The Legend of the 7 Golden Vampires is absolutely preposterous but does what it says on the tin and may have been a little ahead of its time with its mixture of supernatural vampire elements, action and martial arts. It reminds me a bit of Jackie Chan films like Armour of God in spirit and John Carpenter's Big Trouble in Little China - which also threw different genres and elements into one single action packed film.

The Legend of the 7 Golden Vampires general reputation was not helped by some idiot cutting it to pieces and calling it The 7 Brothers Meet Dracula in the United States but this original version is undemanding and enjoyably cheesy seventies blood drenched fun for anyone who has ever wondered what a kung fu vampire film made by Hammer in Hong Kong would turn out like. You get enough impalements, vampire meltdowns, kung fu battles and gratuitous nudity to satisfy most tastes and best of all the great Peter Cushing was roped in to add his customary class and gravitas to this obstreperous nonsense.

Cushing must have been in his sixties by now but still throws himself into the action when required to do so. No one could say lines like "Is the mighty Dracula too frightened to reveal his face to me?" quite like Peter Cushing. Sadly though, Christopher Lee obviously declined this one and was replaced by John Forbes-Robertson which probably explains why Dracula spends most of the film in someone else's body and has about ten minutes of screen time.

Forbes-Robertson's Dracula make-up is awful here and makes him look like a puppet from Captain Scarlet wearing too much lipstick. He's dubbed too by someone with a camp theatrical voice and Dracula's whole presence generally feels like a slight afterthought on the part of the filmmakers as if they'd made a kung fu vampire film and then decided to stick the Dracula name on top to perhaps get a few more bums on seats. Clearly though, you'd rather hear Christopher Lee declare, "I am Dracula! Lord of darkness, master of the vampires, prince of the undead, ruler of the damned!"

No one would argue that The Legend of the 7 Golden Vampires is a particularly good film but it is quite a fun one if you approach it in the right mood. Dracula/Kah has an undead ghoul army to pit against Van Helsing and the kung fu Ching family and - although the make-up is a bit variable - there are some nice moments of these ghouls rising from the grave in battle armour and plenty of action when they do battle with the Van Helsing expedition. The film is more violent than your average Hammer fare and features vats of blood, jugular veins being punctured by martial arts skills, swords, spears and all manner of mayhem.

The "7 Brothers Clan" (who I presume were real life martial artists) are suitably athletic in the film as they leap into action with David Chiang as Hsi Ching and Shih Szu as the sister of the family Mai Kwei both doing a good job in their respective roles. There appears to be no comedy dubbing with these characters either and everyone seems to be speaking English for themselves. Call me cynical but Norwegian actress Julie Ege - who had a tiny bit in the James Bond film On Her Majesty's Secret Service - was probably not cast as Vanessa because of her thesping talents!

The Legend of the 7 Golden Vampires is possibly the most eccentric film Hammer ever made and one that connoisseurs of strange cinema will probably get a kick out of. It has abundant flaws but isn't a film to take too seriously and is likeable for its small scale epic throw the kitchen sink at the screen approach. This is undemanding late night fun and not bad at all.

LIFEFORCE (1985)

We can probably just about claim Lifeforce as a British film because it was a British co-production and made in Britain with many British actors in the cast. Lifeforce is a science fiction horror film directed by Tobe Hooper and written by Dan O'Bannon and Don Jakoby, based on Colin Wilson's 1976 novel The Space Vampires. This was Hooper's first film in his

Cannon Films contract and had a $25 million budget. It practically bankrupted the studio when it failed at the box-office. It's something of a cult film today because it is completely bonkers. It starts in outer space, then becomes a zombie film, a vampire film, an end of the world film. Lifeforce is genuinely insane.

The premise has the crew of the space shuttle Churchill discovering a huge spaceship in Halley's Comet. There are naked humanoids and bat type creatures. They bring the humanoids onboard but this proves to be a fatal error. The Churchill is destroyed and the aliens end up at the European Space Research Centre in London. Well, suffice to say, they eventually reanimate and the female one (memorably played by a naked Mathilda May) escapes. She has the power to drain the 'lifeforce' out of people and turn them into dried up husks who look like zombies. As if that wasn't bad enough she can also shapeshift. Colonel Colin Caine (Colin Firth) of the SAS is brought in to investigate and teams up with the only survivor of the Churchill, Colonel Tom Carlsen (Steve Railsback). Can they save the world from space vampires?

Lifeforce begins in fantastic fashion with Henry Mancini's stirring theme and the Churchill scenes in space. The special effects by John Dykstra are superb. I would say this is the most ambitious film Cannon ever tried to produce. Superman IV doesn't really count because they kept stripping the budget from that. It's a great shame that many of these opening scenes in Lifeforce were cut in the theatrical version. Make sure you watch the longer version. The cast is amazing in this film. Frank Finlay is Dr Hans Fallada at the space centre while Michael Gothard (who you might recognise as a baddie from For Your Eyes Only) is also great as an official at the centre. Patrick Stewart also turns up as the manager of a psychiatric hospital. It's wonderful to see these actors thesping away in such a barmy film.

I love Colin Firth most of all in this film though. Colonel Caine is one of the great unsung heroes of cinema. He's patient, attentive, brave, and resourceful. He manages to accomplish all of his tasks in the film while remaining calm and hardly even taking his coat off! How can you not love the exchange between Firth and Finlay on life after death in this film? Steve Railsback is rather annoying at times though as Carlsen. Rarely have you seen an actor go so completely over the top in a part. Hooper should definitely have got Railsback to tone it down a few notches. To be fair to Railsback, Patrick Stewart does mug his part somewhat too. If you'd have predicted that Stewart would be the next Star Trek captain on the back of Lifeforce they probably would have locked you up.

The scenes where May turns people into mummified zombies by draining their lifeforce are great and the end of the world atmosphere as martial law has been imposed on London makes for a fantastically bizarre last act. The streets are chaotic, zombies mill around, buildings crumble. There's a great bit where Caine and Carsen fight their way to the Prime Minister in a military base but then realise he's become one of the space zombie vampires and beat a hasty retreat. Lifeforce is a tremendously entertaining film that mashes up various genres and fully embraces its brazen madness. It's far from perfect but it has a lot of charm and is the most successful of the three Cannon films that constituted the last chance saloon of Tobe Hooper.

THE LODGER: A STORY OF LONDON FOG (1927)

The Lodger: A Story of the London Fog is a 1927 British silent film directed by Alfred Hitchcock. It is based on the novel of the same name by Marie Belloc Lowndes and is considered one of Hitchcock's earliest masterpieces. The film takes place in 1920s London, where the city is terrorised by a serial killer known as The Avenger, who targets blonde women. A mysterious lodger (played by Ivor Novello) rents a room in a boarding house owned by a young couple, Mr and Mrs

Bunting. As Mr and Mrs Bunting begin to suspect that the lodger may be the notorious killer, tensions rise and a cat-and-mouse game ensues. The killer in the film is a mash-up of Jack the Ripper and Thomas Neill Cream - who became known as The Lambeth Poisoner. In fact, Cream is actually a Ripper suspect (though the fact he was a poisoner - decidedly NOT the Ripper's MO - and was in prison for some of the canonical murders would appear to rule him out).

The book this film is based on was apparently inspired by Dr Forbes Winslow - who claimed to have un masked Jack the Ripper (though he hadn't in reality). Winslow was convinced at one point that the Ripper was Henry Wentworth Bellsmith. Henry Wentworth Bellsmith apparently came to London from Canada in 1888 to work for the Toronto Trust Society. He took some lodgings in Finsbury Square with a Mr and Mrs Callaghan. Though he is often called George in articles it appears that Bellsmith's real name might well have been Henry. He is sometimes reported as being Canadian but was actually English according to most Ripper experts. Anyway, why is Bellsmith of interest in the Ripper case? Well, it appears that his landords the Callaghans became convinced that Bellsmith was none other than Jack the Ripper.

The Callaghans said that Bellsmith was a religious fanatic who was always going on about how prostitutes should be killed and wiped from the streets. They also said that Bellsmith would often make loud moaning noises to himself as if he'd gone into some strange trance. Suffice to say, Mr Bellsmith, it seems, was not the full shilling at this time. The Callaghans allegedly found guns in Bellsmith's drawer - though this seems a moot point as the Ripper didn't use firearms. Many serial killers dislike guns because they destroy the 'intimacy' of murder. Besides, a gun ringing out in Whitechapel in the dead of night would have attracted attention and been reckless. It could be the case that the Ripper didn't have access to a gun anyway.

A more incriminating and interesting find by the Callaghans

was bloodstains on the linen used by Bellsmith. This could have had an innocent explanation but it was definitely odd all the same. They also noted that - rather suspiciously - they once heard Bellsmith creeping back to his room at four in the morning. What on earth could he have been up to at that hour? Mr Callaghan eventually told a certain Dr Forbes Winslow about this dodgy character who had rented a room from him and appeared at first glance to be highly suspicious. Dr Winslow had prestigious qualifications in both law and medicine and his father had run an asylum so he was something of an expert when it came to mental illness. In fact, Winslow was even employed as a court expert to judge the sanity of criminals.

Dr Forbes Winslow looked into the case of this mysterious lodger and became convinced that Bellsmith was Jack the Ripper. As you might imagine, the Callaghans were now more convinced than ever that they were onto something - especially now that they had an expert like Dr Winslow backing them up. The police were notified and in 1889 there was a lot of excitement in the media about how this clever doctor (with a bit of help from the Callaghans) had unmasked Jack the Ripper.

A key detail supplied by Mr Callaghan was that the night on which Bellsmith sneaked back to his lodgings in the early hours was the same night (7 August 1888) that Martha Tabram was murdered. Though not considered one of the canonical 'five', Martha's murder certainly bore the hallmarks of the gruesome handiwork favoured by the Ripper. When you factor all of this together you might think that Bellsmith was a very plausible Ripper suspect. Case closed? Well, not so fast.

The case against Henry Wentworth Bellsmith soon began to weaken upon closer scrutiny. It transpired that Mr Callaghan had either lied or muddled up his dates and Bellsmith's late night disappearance did not occur in conjunction with Martha Tabram's death. It also (later) transpired that Bellsmith was on a steamship when Mary Kelly was murdered. The police investigated the case against Bellsmith and dismissed it. They could find no concrete evidence that he was Jack the Ripper or involved in any of the Whitechapel murders.

It seems that the armchair detective work of Dr Forbes Winslow and the Callaghans proved to be wide of the mark - though to be fair to them they did briefly seem to be onto something at first. This would not be the last time in true crime history that something like this happened. Many decades later, the police already had a suspect in custody when they deduced that Steven Wright was The Suffolk Strangler. The suspect (who was of course innocent) was actually a man suggested to the police by the media pack in East Anglia. The media had noticed this man hanging around a lot and didn't like the look of him. This amateur detective work on the part of the media was very wide of the mark. Like the Bellsmith affair, it was a good example of why detective work should be left to the professionals.

As for Bellsmith, he apparently moved to New York and had some children. Bellsmith is definitely a suspicious and interesting character but it seems that there was never much of a case against him - despite his eccentricities and presence in London at the time of the Ripper era. Dr Winslow did not come out of the Bellsmith affair very well it seems. He was even accused in the press of unfairly giving lodgers a bad name through his zeal to pin the Ripper murders on Bellsmith!

By the way, the police actually became suspicious of Dr Forbes Winslow during this affair and briefly considered the possibility of whether or not he could have been the Ripper. Winslow obviously had medical knowledge, knew Whitechapel, and was familiar with the seedy underbelly of London through his work. What made the police suspicious of Winslow was the way he seemed determined to shoehorn himself into the Ripper investigation and get someone officially named as the killer. One presumes the police had to consider the possibility that this was some sort of misdirection attempt on Winslow's part. In the end though Winslow was not considered to be a serious Ripper suspect. He was simply a local doctor who (like a great many people) had taken an interest in the Ripper case.

Anyway, The Lodger is considered to be one of Hitchcock's greatest silent films. He actually wanted to remake it in the 1940s but he couldn't get the rights. The Lodger showcases Hitchcock's innovative filmmaking techniques, including the use of visual storytelling, dramatic lighting, and suspenseful editing. It explores themes of suspicion, paranoia, and the fear of the unknown, which became recurring motifs in Hitchcock's later works. The film was well received by both critics and audiences at the time of its release. It is often praised for its atmospheric cinematography and its influence on Hitchcock's later films, particularly his fascination with themes of guilt and innocence.

THE MAN WHO HAUNTED HIMSELF (1970)

The Man Who Haunted Himself is a cult 1970 British film directed by Basil Dearden and based on the novel The Strange Case of Mr Pelham by Anthony Armstrong and an episode of Alfred Hitchcock Presents that previously adapted the story. The film is an intriguing and overlooked psychological thriller with a supernatural atmosphere and stars future James Bond actor Roger Moore as a successful but uptight and work obsessed businessman called Harold Pelham. Driving home from his job in the city one afternoon, Pelham has a very bad car accident that leaves him fighting for his life and a strange incident duly occurs in the hospital. Pelham is declared momentarily dead and two hearts briefly flicker on his monitor but he recovers and returns home, eventually resuming his job again after a short break abroad.

Back at work though, some very odd things soon start to occur in Harold's life. Colleagues keep mentioning meetings or conversations they've had with him that Pelham has no memory of whatsoever and he is even told he's apparently agreed to a merger of the company despite being adamant he made no such decision. Pelham is more perplexed than ever when informed he was clearly seen playing billiards in London on a day when he knows for a fact he was recuperating in Spain. As these incidents escalate it almost appears to Pelham that he has a strange double or impostor who always seems to be one step ahead of him and who somehow represents the more wild and suppressed nature of his personality, causing all manner of mayhem to his own life. Is Pelham going mad? The victim of an elaborate practical joke? Or does he really have a malevolent doppelganger attempting to take over his life?

The Man Who Haunted Himself is undoubtedly Roger Moore's finest hour outside of his long stint in the tuxedo and safari suit as James Bond and this likeable and absorbing Twilight Zone style mystery shows that the oft-maligned and rather self-deprecating star was in reality always a lot better than he or anyone else ever gave him credit for when actually required to do some acting. It's no surprise that Moore always spoke of The Man Who Haunted Himself in fond terms and considered it one of his very best roles and pictures.

Roger Moore gives a surprisingly skilful and natural performance here as the increasingly confused and rattled Pelham and makes the plight of the central character both believable and moving at times. It's great to see the actor, in his suave prime just a few years prior to landing the Bond role for 1973's Live and Let Die, in such a dark, eerie and enjoyable film and you just know The Man Who Haunted Himself is going to be a lot of fun right from the start when some funky seventies music opens the film to shots of Roger driving his sleek little sports car past some famous London landmarks.

The car crash that occurs very early in the film is enjoyably strange and slightly delirious as we see Roger Moore looking increasingly nutty and maniacal behind the wheel and dangerously upping his speed on the motorway, hinting at the repression of a personality who is not the staid, ordinary Harold Pelham but a more reckless version. The brief hospital scenes are nicely atmospheric too with a vaguely surreal and psychedelic tinge. In terms of mood, The Man Who Haunted Himself is not a million miles away from one of those episodes of Hammer House of Horror or Hammer House of Mystery and Suspense but much slicker and more polished and without the campy horror elements.

A strength of the film I think is that it seems to use some real locations rather than be too studio bound and constricted. You get a good authentic sense of London and a nice British atmosphere with plenty of shots of the Thames and the pin-striped boardroom shenanigans always feel quite realistic. The world of gentlemen's clubs, billiard rooms, scotches and wood panelling depicted here is quite charming in its own dated way and Roger Moore, with mustache, is certainly believable as a suave well-heeled business type.

The world the film inhabits is an ordinary one and it gives the central mystery more resonance as Pelham's refined and ordered universe begins to be shattered and torn apart. There is a real sense of paranoia in the film at times as Moore struggles to work out what exactly is going on. Other great things about the office and boardroom scenes are Anton Rogers who provides good support as Tony Alexander, Pelham's work colleague and confidant, and Thorley Walters as Pelham's cheery friend Frank.

Basil Dearden, who was of course involved in the supernatural Ealing classic Dead of Night, does a great job here in slowly amping up the tension and psychological strain on Pelham and the film works well by developing at its own pace. I also like the way the film goes for a more realistic approach rather than descend into cheap shocks or straight ahead horror. The Man Who Haunted Himself is genuinely gripping as Pelham's double exerts more and more influence on his life and the sequences where Pelham arrives somewhere and is informed he was already there only minutes previously are suitably creepy.

You are always curious to get to the heart of mystery and follow Pelham as he tries to make sense of it all with the theme of loss of identity an absorbing and slightly unsettling concept here. Most of all though you want Pelham to catch-up with his apparent doppelganger and the film uses this angle very well as Moore's character desperately tries to make their paths cross and meet this strange impostor for himself.

Alastair Mackenzie also does a good job as Moore's wife Eve in the film when the wild antics of the apparent duplicate begin to affect Pelham's home life in various ways. "I'd like to do something reckless," says the bored Eve, who we suspect would find the Pelham doppelganger a lot more interesting than the work obsessed real thing. Roger Moore is very good too in a touching scene where he is utterly bewildered to meet Julie (Olga Georges-Picot), a woman who he has apparently been having an affair with and who knows him well - despite him not having any memory of her whatsoever.

Georges-Picot, who will always be the statuesque Countess Woody Allen comically attempts to seduce in Love and Death to me, is well cast in the film, as is Freddie Jones as Dr Harris, a psychiatrist Pelham consults. The Man Who Haunted Himself is a very entertaining and gripping mystery with a spooky atmosphere and nice direction by Basil Dearden. It has a nice supporting cast, good music and gives Roger Moore his best ever role outside of James Bond. A fun little British film that has been somewhat forgotten over the years and is well worth watching.

MUMSY, NANNY, SONNY, GIRLY (1970)

Mumsy, Nanny, Sonny and Girly (aka 'Girly') was directed by

Freddie Francis and written by Brian Compton. The film is based on a stage play by Maisie Mosco entitled Happy Family. Although this film is rather obscure, Francis considered it to be his best work as a director (this is one of the few films that Francis had complete creative control over - which might explain why he was so fond of it). This is a bizarre horror black comedy and quite possibly a brilliant one too. The film takes place at a grand sprawling country mansion where a family have retreated in a strange old fashioned fantasy world apparently based on children's books. The family are Mumsy (Ursula Howells), Nanny (Pat Heywood), and the children Sonny (Howard Trevor) and Girly (Vanessa Howard).

Although Sonny and Girly wear school uniforms and are treated like children they look rather on the mature side for such treatment. The family play something they call the 'Game'. This involves luring men back to the house - the men then indoctrinated into the rules of the house and forced to behave like children too. If they don't obey the rules they are 'sent to the angels' - in other words they are killed. Whenever a 'friend' is killed, Sonny records it on a camera and they watch the murder on a projector.

This is the sort of film that is better watched then described. It's a strange film but a very compelling one. The tension arises when a man played by Michael Bryant arrives at the house after Sonny and Girly kill his companion (played by Imogen Hassel) in a park by grabbing her foot when she is on top of a slide in a playground. Bryant goes with them to the house to lay low and is blackmailed because they have the body of the woman in the house.

However, Bryant's character observes the family and their bizarre game and concludes that the key to his survival is to get close to Girly. This will create a fracture in the family as Girly won't want to 'share' her new friend - especially when he awakens her sexuality. This is a beautiful looking film (shot at Oakley Court) and amusingly bizarre and deadpan. I gather that Francis was specifically looking for a film he could shoot at Oakley Court and this film was perfect. It makes a wonderful isolated and anachronistic location for this weird family to lurk around in.

There are some good performances in the film but the star is unquestionably Vanessa Howard as Girly. Vanessa Howard is fantastically arch and charismatic and gives a brilliant performance. Vanessa Howard is plainly a star in the making in this film. She has comic charisma to spare and the camera loves her. The tragedy of this film's failure to find an audience, and the subsequent failure of the Amicus film What Became of Jack and Jill?, was that Howard abandoned acting soon afterwards. A terrific shame. Vanessa Howard had no more acting credits after 1973 and moved to the United States, where she married a film producer (Robert Chartoff - who produced the Rocky films) and concentrated on family life.

Mumsy, Nanny, Sonny and Girly bore the brunt of a moral backlash in Blighty due to a scene early on which implies that incest is going on with Girly and Sonny (who are brother and sister). As a consequence of this, few cinemas wanted to show the film. In the United States the title was changed to 'Girly' and the promotional art was focused on Vanessa Howard in her school uniform (Howard was actually 22 when she made this film so it isn't as if she was a real schoolgirl). This tactic worked and the film did quite well in the United States and got some decent reviews. Sadly though, Vanessa Howard was apparently oblivious to this and had no idea the film found a modest audience over there. One nice (if bittersweet) addition to this tale is that an event was held at Oakley Court in 2015 to celebrate the film and a memorial bench to Vanessa Howard (who sadly passed away in 2010) was opened there.

Ursula Howells and Pat Heywood are well cast as Mumsy and Nanny although Howard Trevor, who plays the brother of Girly, is something of a liability and clearly can't act. I'm not completely surprised to see that he didn't have any other acting credits after this film. The only other casting complaint you might have is that the rather plain looking Michael Bryant doesn't really seem like the sort of person who would charm and excite Vanessa Howard but then his performance is very good.

Mumsy, Nanny, Sonny and Girly is a jet black comedy full of memorable scenes and deadpan wit. Though the film is surreal and darkly comic it does get quite bleak too - like the murder at the start and the scene where the family watch a 'snuff' film of a man hunted on the grounds of the house. This surreal darkness of the premise and the brilliant performance by Vanessa Howard make this film well worth watching.

NIGHT OF THE DEMON (1957)

"It has been written since the beginning of time, even unto these ancient stones, that evil supernatural creatures exist in a world of darkness. And it is also said man using the magic power of the ancient runic symbols can call forth these powers of darkness, the demons of Hell."

Night of the Demon is a 1957 British horror film directed by Jacques Tourneur and based on the MR James story Casting the Runes. John Holden (Dana Andrews) is an American scientist who regards the supernatural to be nothing but superstitious nonsense. The work of charlatans. He goes to London to participate in a conference and is informed of the death of Professor Harrington (Maurice Denham). Harrington had been planning to expose an occultist named Karswell (Niall MacGinnis). Holden decides to debunk Karswell himself but as he investigates all manner of strange and spooky events start to plague him...

This is a wonderfully atmospheric little thriller that masterfully uses suspense and the power of suggestion to camouflage its modest budget. Tourneur was famous for his forties horror pictures and uses some of the same techniques to excellent effect. There's a great opening sequence where the first scientist is stalked and killed by the demon and a lot of the tension comes from the dubious Holden's attitude to the supernatural. Will he accept it might all be real in time to save himself?

Holden is well played by Dana Andrews. I suppose Dr Holden is like the Richard Dawkins of his day! "Joanna, let me tell you something about myself. When I was a kid, I used to walk down the street with the other kids and when we came to a ladder they'd all walk around it. I'd walk under it, just to see if anything would happen. Nothing ever did. When they'd see a black cat they'd run the other way to keep it from crossing their path. But I didn't. And all this ever did for me is make me wonder why, why people get so panicky about absolutely nothing at all. I've made a career studying it. Maybe just to prove one thing. That I'm not a superstitious sucker like ninety per cent of humanity."

Niall MacGinnis is terrific as Karswell - making the occultist suave and sinister but also strangely frightened of the forces he can potentially unleash. "But where does imagination end and reality begin? What is this twilight, this half world of the mind that you profess to know so much about? How can we differentiate between the powers of darkness and the powers of the mind?" The acting beyond Andrews and MacGinnis is serviceable but the focus on the duel between these men drives the film.

There are some fine suspenseful scenes in Night of the Demon with chases in the woods, the battle of wits on the train, and a memorable séance scene too. Holden experiences dizzy spells, strange weather, and is attacked by a cat! The demon, when finally revealed, is not terribly convincing and the one false note in the film. I gather that Tourneur was unhappy about this and the demon special effect was a decision by producer Hal E Chester. Tourneur does such a wonderful job in creating dread and chills through suggestion and things unseen so the demon never really needed to be explicitly revealed.

Chester was also responsible for chopping ten minutes from the film and retitling it Curse of the Demon for the American release. You should really watch the longer version as the deliberate and sedate pacing of Night of the Demon is one of its charms. This is a film that unfolds at its own speed and builds layers of atmosphere in a clever fashion. Night of the Demon was a last hurrah for this type of quiet, black and white British horror film as Hammer were on the rise (with colour, blood, and scantily clad women soon to be staples of the genre). Of its type though, Night of the Demon is a superb chiller and still very enjoyable.

PEEPING TOM (1960)

Peeping Tom was directed by Michael Powell and written by Leo Marks. Peeping Tom came out a few months before Alfred Hitchcock's Psycho - a film it shares some similarities with in that it was shocking for its time and revolves around a strange, shy young man who seems quite innocuous at first glance but is actually very dangerous. The reception of the two films was very different though. Psycho got a lot of praise and was a big success - whereas Peeping Tom was trashed by British critics and damaged Michael Powell's career.

It is said that when Hitchcock saw the critical reception to Peeping Tom he axed the critic screenings for Psycho to avoid any advance reviews. It seems a bit unfair really that Peeping Tom got such a rocky reception. It may have been because Michael Powell was one of Britain's greatest directors and critics thought he was 'slumming it' by making a seedy thriller film like this. Peeping Tom is a very stylish film but few seemed to acknowledge this. It appears that critics were put off by the subject matter.

These days Peeping Tom is regarded to be a classic film that was simply a bit ahead of its time. Some would argue that the slasher genre in horror actually has its roots in Peeping Tom.

Peeping Tom goes beyond traditional horror tropes, using voyeurism as a metaphor for the invasive nature of filmmaking itself. The story in Peeping Tom revolves around Mark Lewis (Carl Boehm), a soft-spoken and unassuming cameraman who, unbeknownst to everyone, hides a chilling secret. Aside from his day job, Mark indulges his voyeuristic tendencies, capturing the last moments of women's terror as he films them, ultimately resulting in their gruesome murders. He literally films the last moments of people as he kills them.

As the story unfolds, we witness the twisted psyche of a seemingly ordinary man unravel, leading to a climax filled with suspense and horror. The film delves deep into the psychological aspects of voyeurism. It highlights the protagonist's compulsion to film murders and his obsession with watching the fear in his victims' eyes. Michael Powell's direction in Peeping Tom is very inventive. He expertly employs unique camera angles and subjective shots to place the audience directly in Mark's shoes, intensifying the suspense and unease. The choice to shoot in Technicolor, unusual for a British horror film of its time, amplifies the vividness of the visuals, further immersing the audience in Mark's twisted world.

Additionally, Powell delves into themes of psychoanalysis, exploring the psychological impact of a traumatic childhood. By exploring Mark's upbringing as a guinea pig for his father's disturbing experiments, the film suggests that our past experiences can shape our destructive tendencies. The film also explores the connection between art and obsession. The protagonist is a cinema cameraman who is obsessed with capturing fear on film. His obsession with creating art through his murders blurs the lines between reality and his artistic vision. Through the use of his camera, Mark Lewis objectifies women, reducing them to subjects of his voyeuristic desires. Peeping Tom was deemed very shocking when it was released and even banned in some countries. Today the film is considered to be a masterpiece of psychological horror.

Carl Boehm is effective enough in the lead and Anna Massey deserves a mention as the kind neighbour who Mark befriends. Apparently they wanted Dirk Bogarde for the lead in Peeping Tom but he couldn't do it because he was contracted to another studio. That would have been a shock for audiences who only knew Dirk Bogarde for the Doctor films! I think Peeping Tom would be even more of a cult classic today if Dirk Bogarde had been in it (and Bogarde loved edgy parts so there is no reason why he wouldn't have done it).

Peeping Tom is a happy example of a film that didn't get a fair reception at the time later getting the love it deserved. No lesser figure than Martin Scorsese has called Peeping Tom one of the most important films ever made.

PSYCHOMANIA (1973)

Psychomania was directed by Don Sharp. The film was made by the same production company as Horror Express. Is there anything more British and 1970s than the unconvincing film motorcycle ruffian? Well, Psychomania is the ultimate unconvincing motorcycle ruffian film. The tearaways in this film are supposed to be highly dangerous bikers and a threat to society but half of them sound suspiciously like they've come straight from a posh stage school rather than a broken home. Not that I'm complaining about any of this mind you because Psychomania is an awful lot of fun and powered by a funky catchy score by John Cameron which will rattle around in your head for days afterwards.

The story in Psychomania concerns a biker gang known as The Living Dead. The leader of this gang is a young rebel named Tom (Nicky Henson). What exactly Tom has to rebel against is anyone's guess because he lives in a plush house the size of an embassy and his family even has a butler named Shadwell (George Sanders). Shadwell is no ordinary butler though. He's very mysterious and occult. It transpires that Tom's mother

Mrs Latham (Beryl Reid) made a pact with a Frog God (or something) and when Tom learns that the dead return to life if they really believe they will return (this is the important part, you HAVE to believe you will come back - otherwise it won't work) he commits suicide.

Tom then rides (quite literally) out of the grave on his motorcycle and is delighted because he is now superhuman and can't be killed. So he, as you do, does all the things he's ever wanted to do - like speed through a brick wall and ride his bike through a supermarket knocking cans of soup all over the place. Anyway, Tom implores his biker gang to all commit suicide and come back from the dead so they can be just like him and all do anything they want. For all eternity they'll be able to ride their motorbikes through supermarkets knocking tins of soup all over the place and there'll be nothing that anyone can do about it. There is only one problem though. Abby (Mary Larkin), a member of the gang who Tom is very sweet on, isn't very keen on committing suicide and Chief Inspector Hesseltine (Robert Hardy), who is on the trail of these motorcycle hooligans, decides he might be able to use Abby to his advantage.

Psychomania is quite eerie in places but it's fairly tame as a horror film. There isn't really much gore or violence in the film. It is tremendously entertaining though and all the chases and bike riding sequences are very well done. The film has a fantastic opening with the gang riding their bikes around megalithic stones in the mist. This stone circle is called The Seven Witches and is where the gang like to hang out when they take a break from trying to run over pensioners and pushchairs in shopping arcades. The antics of the motorcycle gang are done in such a silly way that you can't take their anti-social activities very seriously. The film is so much fun though that it doesn't matter in the least and there's never a dull stretch either. The sequences where the bikers commit suicide (in increasingly elaborate ways - including skydiving!) are highly entertaining.

The actual plot of this film is a trifle on the vague side when it comes to the occult mumbo jumbo but the scenes with Beryl Reid and George Sanders in the arty decor house are arrestingly odd and allow the film to take a break from the motorcycle shenanigans now and again. Sadly, this was Sanders last film - he committed suicide not long after Psychomania. I gather that George Sanders shot all of his scenes inside six days as fast as possible because they couldn't afford to hire him for any longer. Beryl Reid plays it fairly straight in the film but you can definitely see a twinkle in her eyes - she KNOWS this is a daft film and is trying not to laugh.

Nicky Henson, a cheeky chappie sort of actor who was in everything from Fawlty Towers to Minder to Eastenders, is a bit miscast as Tom in that Tom is supposed to be a murderous detestable nihilist. Henson is a trifle too ordinary and likeable to make the most of this character (someone like Jon Finch would have made Tom sinister and unlikeable - which might have worked better) but it isn't a major drawback. To the credit of Henson, he isn't phoning it in or playing down to the material. He's actually taking it seriously and giving a straight performance. Robert Hardy as the police inspector on the trail of the bikers never hams it up as much as you hope but I did enjoy his Yorkshire accent.

There are a couple of familiar faces among the supporting cast like Bill Pertwee and Dot Cotton from Eastenders. Mary Larkin is likeable as Abby (Larkin's acting career seemed to become sporadic after the 1970s but she has been in things like Casualty and Eastenders in more recent years). There are some murders in the film but there isn't any gore and the horror elements only really come at the end. The seance sequence which opens the film and the Frog God capers near the end do add a nice element of the supernatural. Psychomania is a fairly unique sort of experience. It is kitschy, tongue in cheek, has crazy enjoyable stunts, a bizarre plot, and even has a folk song interlude during Tom's funeral.

While this is plainly a silly film, it is made with style and panache on a non-existent budget. Psychomania is an interesting film in this period opf British horror because it is trying to do something different from the usual period Gothic horror capers. It is trying to be hip and modern. While it is a bit risible in places, Psychomania is a delight today with its fantastic score, location work, exciting chases scenes, black comedy, and throw the kitchen sink in attitude to giving the audience a good time. If you have a weakness for 1970s British horror films and like motorcycles then you really have no excuse not to embrace the weird and crazy world of Psychomania.

QUATERMASS AND THE PIT (1967)

Quatermass and the Pit (aka Five Million Years to Earth) is a science fiction horror film from Hammer, a sequel to the earlier Hammer films The Quatermass Xperiment and Quatermass 2. Like its predecessors it is based on a BBC Television serial – Quatermass and the Pit – written by Nigel Kneale. It was directed by Roy Ward Baker. In the London underground system, some construction work is being undertaken to a tunnel at Hobb's End. Skeletons are discovered and archaeologist Dr Mathew Roney (James Donald) is asked to investigate this strange discovery. Roney and his assistant Barbara Judd (Barbara Shelley) are intrigued that the skeletons are not Homo sapiens.

A mysterious metallic object is then discovered and taken to be an un exploded World War 2 bomb. The area where the station is being built has a troubled and spooky history - the houses in the area have been left unoccupied since before the War with the previous tenants complaining of mysterious apparitions. Meanwhile, Quatermass (Andrew Keir) is having trouble with the government - who want to turn his moon-base research over to the military, so he is required to work with the stubborn Colonel Breen (Julian Glover). Breen and Quatermass are sent to Hobb's End to look into the puzzling situation and unearth what seems to be an alien spacecraft of some sort. It contains a secret that could spell disaster for the human race.

Quatermass and the Pit is one of the most famous Hammer films and still works well today. It's a typically dense Nigel Kneale tale involving telekinesis, aliens, missing links, genetic meddling, the devil, science versus the supernatural, and more besides. The film is very atmospheric in the underground scenes as they try to enter the small alien vessel. I always felt sorry for the poor workman who tries (unsuccessfully at first) to drill his way in because later they seem to leave him alone down there and he goes doolally! They do make the dig site down in the bowels of the underground very creepy. If you've ever used one of the very deep tube stations in London like Russell Square you'll be aware of the very strange aura that comes from going deep underground. Even with people and trains down there they can be weird places so imagine them empty.

Julian Glover is great as the no nonsense military man who thinks it's all a German ruse! I love the idea that years after the war he still hasn't quite accepted that the Nazis are done and dusted! Colonel Breen thinks that little green men from outer space are a preposterous notion. Nazis seem more plausible. Quatermass slowly pieces together the real story. An alien civilisation perished on earth but left their thoughts in the subconscious of humans. This could mean big trouble. If you ever wondered where the 'London in chaos' sequence at the end of Tobe Hopper's Lifeforce came from, well Quatermass and the Pit is the obvious source.

Maybe the aliens (essentially oversized insects) are somewhat hokey now but it's part of the charm. You've seen better special effects in sixties films but - generally - the acting and Nigel Kneale's story still hold up very well indeed and make this a compelling film perfect for late night viewing. Quatermass and the Pit is one of those films that you always find yourself watching again when it comes on television - even if you already have the DVD. It has a fine cast and a rich supernatural atmosphere of doom.

REPULSION (1965)

Repulsion is a psychological horror film directed by Roman Polanski. The film is set in London and follows the story of Carol (Catherine Deneuve), a young woman who gradually descends into madness and experiences hallucinations and delusions. Carol becomes increasingly repulsed by men and develops an extreme aversion towards sexual encounters. As her mental state deteriorates, her isolation and paranoia intensify, leading to violent outbursts.

Polanski expertly employs various elements to immerse the viewers into Carol's deteriorating mental state. The film's unconventional cinematography, featuring extreme close-ups, distorted angles, and disorienting shots, effectively echoes Carol's distorted perception of reality. The use of silence within the film highlights the protagonist's isolation and intensifies the eerie atmosphere, engrossing the audience in her increasingly disordered world.

One of the most striking aspects of Repulsion is its meticulous attention to detail and symbolism. The decaying apartment that Carol occupies slowly becomes a physical manifestation of her unstable mental state, with peeling wallpaper and rotting food strewn about, reinforcing her inner turmoil. The use of mirrors throughout the film brilliantly reflects Carol's shattered psyche, often blurring the boundaries between reality and her hallucinatory experiences. The film's soundtrack plays a vital role in heightening the sense of unease and tension. Challenging traditional horror scores, composer Chico Hamilton manages to create an unsettling and haunting soundscape, using a mixture of jarring dissonance, oppressive silence, and distorted sounds. The score perfectly complements the dark and disturbing visuals, ensuring an infernal fusion of sight and sound.

Polanski's direction in Repulsion is highly inventive. He masterfully builds suspense and unnerving atmosphere, gradually increasing the intensity until it reaches a climax that leaves viewers on the edge of their seats. The use of minimal dialogue draws attention to the characters' actions and expressions, allowing the audience to interpret their emotions and motives for themselves. Thematically, Repulsion delves deep into the dark recesses of the human mind. It explores the consequences of societal pressure, sexual repression, and trauma, and raises questions about the fragile nature of sanity. Polanski manages to craft a narrative that transcends a simple horror story, leaving viewers with a profound and lasting impression.

There's a great cast too in Repulsion with a major role for Ian Hendry. Look out too for Randall & Hopkirk star Mike Pratt in a blink and you'll miss it part. One of the great things about this film is the authentic location work - which makes everything seem more realistic. They look like they shot everything in real places (as opposed to studio sets). This was the first English language film by Polanski and although Repulsion came very early in his career it is still considered to be one of his best films along with Chinatown and Rosemary's Baby.

SCREAM AND SCREAM AGAIN (1970)

Scream and Scream Again was directed by Gordon Hessler and written by Christopher Wicking. It is based on the novel The Disorientated Man by Peter Saxon. Scream and Scream Again is - famously - absolutely bonkers. This is often more of a surreal thriller than a horror film despite the wonderfully melodramatic (and very Amicus) pulp title. It all begins with a jogger ambling through London as the titles roll. The jogger has what appears to be a heart attack and wakes up in a private hospital room where he's being attended to by a nurse who doesn't talk much. Doesn't sound too bad I suppose. All except for one thing. Each time he wakes up he seems to be missing another limb! What on earth is going on?

Meanwhile, in an unknown Eastern European country, where some sort of fascist government seems to be in power, intelligence operative Konartz (Marshall Jones) is given a briefing by his superior, who is no lesser figure than Cleggy from Last of the Summer Wine (aka actor Peter Sallis). Konartz promptly gives Cleggy a Vulcan neck pinch, killing him almost instantly. And as far as plot threads in Scream and Scream Again go, last, but by no means least, we have a killer on the loose in London. The killer seems to be a shaggy haired Michael Gothard in a purple shirt. The sarcastic Police Superintendent Bellaver (Alfred Marks) is assigned to the case.

Scream and Scream Again is a tremendously confusing film the first time you watch it. You have all these different plot threads all jumbled together and none of them seem to make any sense. Really though, that turns out to be the main charm of the film - the outrageously eccentric 'throw the kitchen sink' at the story approach to it all. To be fair, they do tie everything together at the end and while it still doesn't make sense at least they tried!

The presence of horror icons Christopher Lee, Peter Cushing, and Vincent Price in the same film is (sadly) somewhat misleading. All have minor roles (Cushing vanishes after one scene where he plays a leader in the totalitarian state and gets a Vulcan death pinch from Konartz). Price appears a few times as a mad doctor named Dr Browning experimenting in transplants, and Lee plays a small part as a snooty and mysterious intelligence bigwig named Fremont. The only time any of them share a scene is at the end when Lee and Price appear together but it doesn't last for very long and you barely seem them in the same frame. It's a shame really that none of these legends appear for longer or share any notable scenes.

Much of the screen time then rests on Alfred Marks as the no nonsense Superintendent Bellaver. Marks (who apparently improvised his dialogue) is quite funny and droll in the film. He's rather like Donald Pleasance in the (later) British horror film Death Line. Interestingly, Christopher Lee also played a mysterious and snooty intelligence/government bigwig in that film too. He's essentially playing the same character here in Scream and Scream Again that he played in Death Line.

Scream and Scream Again mitigates the haphazard nature of the plot with plenty of action and an upbeat poppy music score. There's a long sequence where Michael Gothard is chased by the police (for what seems like forever) that is really well directed. There's none of the terrible back projection you usually get in films of this era when they have car chase sequences. This is a tyre screeching car chase on a real road. It's great fun. The police keep getting duffed up by Gothard too when they try to apprehend him as he's supposed to be superhuman. I must say though, that the police don't show too much evidence of street smarts when they handcuff him to a car and then wander off to have a chat. If someone had just beaten up a dozen coppers and displayed superhuman strength I'd probably want to keep a closer eye on him!

The third act finds Scream and Scream Again shifting into another gear and has Christopher Matthews as Dr David Sorel becoming the main character as he seeks to understand what exactly is going on - a desire greatly shared by the audience!

It feels like there are three or four separate films in Scream and Scream Again all jostling together and fighting one another for space. It all swings back to Vincent Price in the last act as the mad doctor. If someone HAS to explain the plot and give a grand speech at the end of Scream and Scream Again, then I can think of no one better than Vincent Price to perform this duty!

Scream and Scream Again is a really bizarre film that is difficult to describe. It doesn't make an awful lot of sense and the various plot strands in the first half don't even seem to belong in the same film let alone mesh together but somehow, miraculously, it all sort of works in the end. Scream and Scream Again has grown in stature over the years and even become something of a cult film. There has never been anything quite like it before or since, this strange blending of different story arcs, genres, and characters.

One minute you've got Peter Cushing in what looks like an SS uniform and then we're at a London disco or something. You never know what to expect next in Scream and Scream Again and that's the secret of its charm and entertainment factor. There's a fine cast, plenty of action, good direction, some shocks, twists and turns, and a general aura of surreal insanity and unpredictability that quickly makes you want to stop nitpicking and just surrender yourself to the enjoyable madness that is Scream and Scream Again.

SEVERANCE (2006)

Severance is a 2006 comic horror film co-written and directed by Christopher Smith. This film is notable for featuring what I consider to be the quintessential Danny Dyer performance. Now, you might think that is damning with faint praise because this is the man who was in Run for Your Wife. However, Danny Dyer is fun in this film. He's actually a great unconventional leading man in Severance. His character is so drug addled he barely knows where he is half the time but he still ends up becoming an action hero when the you know what hits the fan.

What is the plot of Severance? The sales division of a weapons company travel to a remote part of Hungary to take part in a team bonding exercise at a rural lodge. The team is made up of the manager Richard (Tim McInnerny), Harris (Toby Stephens), the nerdy Gordon (Andy Nyman), Maggie (Laura Harris), the permanently drugged up Steve (Danny Dyer), Jill

(Claudie Blakley), and Billy (Babou Ceesay). How did Steve get all these drugs through customs? And doesn't this company have drug testing for its employees? Sorry, I'm nitpicking. Let's get back to the plot.

When the road is blocked by a fallen tree, the coach driver refuses to go any further through the woods so the office workers make their way to the lodge on foot. When they get there though it is a ramshackle place and contains strange Russian documents which hint at sinister secrets. Is this the actual lodge or are they in the wrong place? Well, no prizes for guessing the correct answer to that question. This is a horror film so bad things are bound to happen and being in the wrong place is merely the start. It soon transpires that someone has a vendetta against the company these workers are employed by and everyone is in great danger.

It is probably inaccurate to call this film a horror comedy because the horror and gore is quite brutal at times. This is actually a very effective horror film in the way it puts you on edge and develops an aura of danger. It is essentially a full blooded horror film but a full blooded horror film that has a good sense of humour. It helps a lot in Severance that there's a very talented cast here who all bounce off one another and help lift the material up a few notches. Without this cast it could be the case that Severance wouldn't have worked nearly as well.

This film is quite interesting in that it came out during the height of the 'torture porn' (as it was dubbed) era and Severance sort of feels like a British twist on that genre. I'm not personally the biggest fan of horror films like the Hostel and Saw franchises. They just aren't really my cup of tea. I did enjoy the slightly more comedic take on this sort of film you get with Severance though. There are plenty of laughs in the film but it won't be for the faint hearted either. Gordon gets his leg caught in a bear trap, there are decapitations, a high body count, and the villains - mostly unseen military types - are terrifying.

Severance is generally well judged in that it is a grisly film but a witty one too and this mitigates the nastiness and makes you laugh WITH the film's enjoyably nasty moments. The only ill judged sequence for me comes when one of the characters is doused in petrol and set alight. This sequence comes off as too much, too mean spirited, and doesn't mesh with the balanced nature of the rest of the film - where the deaths or grisly moments contain humour. Severance is clever in that way that it loops back to the prologue (which features two young women trapped in a pit) and is full of surprising and funny moments of black comedy - the airliner scene a case in point.

Danny Dyer is actually very charismatic in this film as Steve and his bloody fights with the shadowy villains are well staged. Laura Harris is also good as what is essentially the leading lady part. Having good comic pros like Tim McInnerny and Andy Nyman in the cast reaps some rich dividends when it comes to the more comedic aspects of the film. Severance is one of those films where you don't go in expecting much (especially as the plot sounds so familiar) but it turns out to be surprisingly funny and surprisingly entertaining. This film, if you ask me, is a cut above many of the British horror films that have abounded since of the turn of the century and a lot of that has to do with the shrewd casting and the way the violence is offset by a sense of humour.

SHAUN OF THE DEAD (2004)

Shaun of the Dead is a zombie comedy film directed by Edgar Wright and written by Wright and Simon Pegg. Who hasn't seen Shaun of the Dead by now? It is rightly regarded to be one of the best modern horror comedies. A wave of dire British horror comedies followed in its wake (everything from Doghouse to Lesbian Vampire Killers to Cockneys vs Zombies to Strippers vs Werewolves and so on) but none of them could get anywhere near capturing the magic and invention of Shaun of the Dead.

They say imitation is the most sincere form of flattery and an untold number of British horror comedies tried to ride the coattails Shaun of the Dead. I'd imagine few people can remember many of these films today. It isn't easy doing a comedic horror film. It is difficult to think of many great ones. Return of the Living Dead and Evil Dead II are the ones that spring to mind most readily. The secret in both of these examples is that they are well made full blooded horror films which are witty and funny too. It's a difficult thing to pull off.

Shaun of the Dead, as if you didn't know, has Simon Pegg as Shaun. Shaun works in a Currys style electrics shop and is drifting along in life going nowhere fast. His girlfriend Liz (Kate Ashfield) is frustrated by his lack of ambition and the fact that he'd rather go down the Winchester pub with his slacker housemate Ed (Nick Frost) than do anything new or romantic. It turns out though that London is in the grip of a zombie epidemic - but will Shaun and Ed even notice?

Why does Shaun of the Dead succeed where all those other horror comedies failed? Well, it obviously has a lot to do with having Edgar Wright behind the camera. Wright is an endlessly inventive director with a distinctive editing style and he does wonders here on a modest budget. The script by Wright and Pegg is also clever and witty. Shaun of the Dead was the first part of Three Flavours Cornetto trilogy - which later included Hot Fuzz and The World's End. I find that the films Edgar Wright later made away from Simon Pegg lack the cleverness and wit of the Cornetto films. They don't have the same depth. Sure, they still look great but they feel all surface gloss and shallow compared to Shaun of the Dead or The World's End.

Shaun of the Dead also has a terrific cast. Dylan Moran and Lucy Davis know their way around a comedy script while Bill Nighy and Penelope Wilton add some (comic) gravitas as Shaun's step-father and mother respectively. Simon Pegg gives one of his best performances here and makes Shaun, as flawed as he might be, a character we root for and Nick Frost is perfectly cast as the bumbling Ed - the archetypal slacker. There's a great moment in Shaun of the Dead where the characters basically meet what could have been an alternative cast for the film - with Martin Freeman, Reece Shearsmith, Matt Lucas and others. Shaun of the Dead has every comic actor you can think of making an appearance.

What helps the film too is that this is genuinely a love letter to George Romero. The zombies are good and the gore is full on when it arrives. To mesh a very British comedy into a Romero type universe is an idea that could have gone disastrously wrong but it works brilliantly. There are many nice little horror in-jokes in Shaun of the Dead too. Shaun works at 'Foree Electric'. This is a reference to Dawn of the Dead star Ken Foree. Fulci's Restaurant is a reference to Italian horror director Lucio Fulci. Shaun of the Dead cost $4 million to make and grossed $30 million. George Romero was a big fan of the film and gave Simon Pegg and Edgar Wright cameos in Land of the Dead as zombies.

The film runs out of steam a bit when they hole up in the Winchester but it has a great punchline and you get more than enough horror and laughs to satisfy. It's a nice idea to have Shaun not even notice the zombie epidemic at first because most of us are oblivious to things outside of our own little mundane bubble at the best of times. And many of us tend to avoid watching the news more and more as we get older because it's so depressing! Shaun of the Dead is one of those films you can watch over and over again. If it turns up on television you often find yourself watching it no matter how many times you've seen it before and that's about the highest praise you can give any film.

THE SKULL (1965)

The Skull was directed by Freddie Francis and written by Milton Subotsky. It is based on the short story by Robert Bloch

- The Skull of the Marquis de Sade. Freddie Francis said that much of Subotsky's original script was jettisoned and rewritten while they were shooting the film. The story revolves around an antiques collector named Christopher Maitland (Peter Cushing) who has a particular interest in rare and unusual objects of the occult.

Maitland is offered the chance to possess the skull of the Marquis de Sade by the dodgy dealer Marco (Patrick Wymark). It transpires that the skull was stolen from Maitland's friend Sir Matthew Phillips (Christopher Lee). Phillips was very happy to be rid of it though for this dangerous and devilish skull is cursed and seems to spell madness and doom for anyone who dares to come into contact with it. "All I can say to you is keep away from the skull of the Marquis de Sade!" The unwitting Maitland is about to find this all out for himself. Never meddle with things you don't understand in horror films. It can only lead to trouble. Will Maitland be able to offer any resistance to the diabolical curse of the skull?

The Skull is an absorbing and wonderfully acted horror film with a terrific cast of actors. Although it is boosted by a strange and atmospheric score by Elisabeth Lutyens, one of the interesting things about the film is the way too that it also isn't afraid of silence. There are long scenes and sequences that play out with just Cushing onscreen alone and they are all very compelling. This is definitely a film you should never casually watch as something on in the background. You have to always pay close attention and watch each and every scene because parts of the story are conveyed in a very visual way with little to no dialogue.

One clever touch in The Skull is the way that the film begins in the 1800s with the grave of the Marquis de Sade plundered and said graverobber then meeting a nasty end for his trouble. We therefore assume this is going to be a period film that mimics Hammer but once this prologue ends we move to the present day with Cushing's antiques collector. It's a nice little way to whip the rug out from under the expectations of the viewer. Amicus show us they are perfectly capable of making a Hammer horror type of film but then quickly move away and give us something slightly different. The 'present day' in the film feels enjoyably anachronistic though, a quality which Amicus and horror films in general often have.

Once in the present day, the focus of the story is Cushing and he's very good in this film as you would expect. It's nice to have an Amicus film where Cushing is the lead in what is a relatively 'straight' role. Maitland isn't an eccentric or a doddery old man. He's quite a thoughtful and intelligent man but fairly normal. Just Cushing sitting alone and quietly musing on this puzzling mystery in his occult antique and book strewn home is great fun. I would love to live in Maitland's house from The Skull. It looks like an ancient but stylish and very cosy Victorian book shop. Cushing always engages our curiosity in the story and is also believably terrified when the skull begins to exert its dark powers. As a character, Maitland (Milton Subotsky was strangely obsessed with the name 'Maitland' wasn't he?) is a good window through which the story is told.

Christopher Lee, in a glorified cameo, only has a few scenes in the film but he makes the most of them and it's always a pleasure to see Cushing and Lee together onscreen. Look out for the scene where they seem to having a frame of snooker (or billiards perhaps). You can tell that Christopher Lee is no Jimmy White. The shot he plays is terrible! There's a fun scene too at the start of The Skull where Lee's character begins making ludicrously over inflated bids at an auction - much to the bafflement of Maitland. You could easily imagine Lee and Cushing swapping roles in The Skull and both being equally effective. It's nice though to have Cushing as the lead here as he often played the supporting role of the friend in many of these types of films.

The highlight of the film comes when the curse of the skull starts to have grave consequences for Cushing and exert a hypnotic trippy effect of bizarre nightmarish imagery. Maitland is arrested (by patently bogus policemen) and put through a surreal Kafkaesque ordeal full of nightmare fuel. It's great stuff. The scene where Cushing is arrested and sits in the back of a car with these sullen heavies who claim to be detectives is very good too. The Skull is quite constrictive and mostly plays out in a few rooms and buildings but it doesn't really matter because the intimate nature of the piece is very compelling. This is one horror film where the budget (and, as we know, Amicus never had a huge amount of money to juggle with when it came to making films) isn't a problem as there are not really any monsters or elaborate set designs and special effects in The Skull.

There are some great little cameos in The Skull that make it even more cultish and enjoyable. Michael Gough appears as an auctioneer at the start and the barking mad Patrick Magee has a small part as a police doctor. Magee only has a few scenes but it's great to see him anyway. Nigel Green (of Zulu fame) also has a few cameo appearances as a stern by the book police inspector investigating the strange events that abound in the wake of the skull. The last act of the film is enjoyably strange and delirious as the frazzled Maitland feels the full brunt of the curse. Those shots of Cushing 'through' the perspective of the skull are a little hokey but great fun.

The Skull is a good little horror picture that is a must watch for Cushing fans - and who isn't a fan of Peter Cushing? The only possible drawback for some might be the slow burn nature of the mystery and the lack of spectacle and blood. Those who do appreciate the slow pacing and use of silence will find much to enjoy though in this film though.

The Skull is a very enjoyable little horror mystery and is all the more enjoyable for the leading part it affords the great Peter Cushing.

THE STONE TAPE (1972)

The Stone Tape is a spooky 1972 BBC television play directed by Peter Sasdy and written by Nigel Kneale of Quatermass fame. Like Jonathan Miller's BBC MR James adaption Whistle And I'll Come To You, The Stone Tape was first shown at Christmas and is both fondly remembered and generally regarded to be one of the more scary things transmitted on British television over the years. Kneale once again presents us with an interesting blend of science-fiction and the supernatural in this inventive tale which has an electronics company (Ryan Electronics) attempting to restore Britain's flagging prestige in this economic field by inventing a new type of recording medium to replace magnetic tape and put one over on the Japanese. They renovate a creaky old haunted Victorian mansion to turn into a research facility for their experiments and place it under the control of abrasive team leader Peter Brock (Michael Bryant).

"Give me Wagner's Ring Cycle encoded onto a ball baring with instant playback," barks Brock. When they arrive at the new facility though, the team are soon warned by foreman Roy Collinson (Iain Cuthbertson) about an uncompleted and unsettling room in the house that the builders staunchly refused to work in. Brock investigates the room (which was supposed to be their computer area) with Jill Greeley (Jane Asher), a computer programmer attuned to psychic phenomena, and they discover dusty tins of spam left by soldiers stationed there during the war and a letter written to Father Christmas long ago by an Edwardian girl. "What I want for Christmas is please go away!"

When Brock discovers a stone staircase behind a wood panel, Jill lingers in the room for a moment afterwards and sees the apparition of a Victorian maid running up the stairs, screaming and falling to her death. Believing the ghost to be a psychic impression in the stone walls - or a "stone tape" - the ambitious Brock decides to investigate for the purposes of their research. "Let's say it's a mass of data waiting for a correct interpretation," he suggests. The team move into the haunted room with their high-tech equipment to work out the secrets of this stone tape but are they foolishly meddling with dark and ancient forces they don't truly understand?

Despite the modest budget/production values and rudimentary special effects, The Stone Tape still works surprisingly well and is both consistently creepy and absorbing with an excellent script by Nigel Kneale and some decent performances from the cast. There is a real sense of unease throughout and the story is intricate and layered with wonderfully weird electronic sounds, hums and beeps by the BBC Radiophonic Workshop to convey the electrical equipment of the team and the doom laden atmosphere of the house.

The opening green title sequence, over oscillator wave-forms, is suitably strange, spare and ominous. Kneale considers in The Stone Tape whether ghosts - should they exist - are sentient with the ability to interact with us or merely a specific moment in time captured in a psychic impression, endlessly repeating themselves like a tape does whenever you switch it on. "Does she walk when nobody's there?" muses Jill. The haunted room was meant to be Jill's computer space but she finds only cobwebs and rotting floorboards on arrival - this emphasising her alienation from the team despite being possibly their most competent member. Brock is furious at the room not being prepared for them and stomps around tearing things down, leading to some very old and startling discoveries.

Michael Bryant is excellent as the boorish and brash Brock and seems more interested in his work than his team's well-being. We see Brock, although married, involved with Jill in the story only to coldly distance himself when she becomes ever more troubled by the vision of the maid she saw. Brock is a cad who is blind to Jill's mental deterioration, her experience initially dismissed as an aural hallucination.

Jane Asher is well cast too with the growing void between Jill and Brock nicely played by the two actors. Asher is adept at reacting to things and acting scared and proves to have a good pair of lungs in the play's third act. The climax is a memorable and scary one and, oddly enough, the basic, shapeless seventies visual effects if anything make it even more unsettling. The staircase Brock discovers is a remnant of a much older structure - possibly from Saxon times. Brock, who is like an early Thatcherite, is rather upset because if anyone discovers this then the historic nature of the find might soon place it off-limits to both him and Ryan Electronics. The key to the story is the hubris and ambition of Brock.

It's fun to watch the Ryan team - with their clunky early seventies Dr Who style equipment - attempting to gain a scientific grasp on these ghostly events. They set up camp in the room and monitor activities with cameras, microphones, sound tapes and video monitors, Brock blasting the room with gigantic speakers at one point in an attempt to provoke the haunting, trying to trigger the manifestation with high-frequency sound.

When they try to measure the physical manifestations of the haunting with their dated high-tech gadgets they have no luck and conclude this is a psychological recording, stored in the surroundings and played into their minds. They may have found exactly what they were looking for - a new type of recording medium - and Brock immediately sets the team to work again as they become increasingly frazzled by his attitude and the ghostly screams that pierce the stone walls periodically.

Jill even starts to worry that the maid screaming in her apparition may be trapped in the haunting, forced to live these moments over and over again. The film takes us away from the research occasionally into Hammeresque territory with characters from the local village dispensing warnings about the house - which Ryan have renamed Tasklands. Parish records, death reports, and newspaper clippings begin to slowly come together to indicate an ancient and terrifying phenomenon and Brock becomes increasingly unhinged and desperate as he seeks to show Ryan results.

This fusion of the traditional into a story about science makes for an enjoyable mix. Corporate humour is also provided in the script by Brock's funding being threatened by another Ryan Electronics project - an intelligent washing machine! Despite the dated elements this is still a genuinely spooky and unsettling ghost story with a veneer of science-fiction. The ending in particular is wonderful.

THEATRE OF BLOOD (1973)

Theatre of Blood was directed by Douglas Hickox. This film has a killer premise. Vincent Price plays a hammy Shakespearean actor named Edward Lionheart who, after getting dreadful reviews and being humiliated at a critic's awards, fakes his own death and then seeks revenge on these snooty critics who mocked his acting. He decides to murder them using methods taken from Shakespeare's plays! Aiding him in this grisly plan is his daughter Edwina (Diana Rigg) and an underground gang of drunken vagrants - to whom Lionheart frequently performs his legendary (or so he thinks) thesping skills to.

As if Vincent Price and Diana Rigg wasn't enough, there is an amazing supporting cast in Theatre of Blood. Jack Hawkins, Harry Andrews, Robert Morley, Michael Hordern, Ian Hendry, Robert Coote, Arthur Lowe, Dennis Price, Coral Browne. You also get Milo O'Shea and Eric Sykes as the police officers and even Diana Dors and Madeline Smith make an appearance. Who could ask for more?

Theatre of Blood is often called an unofficial Dr Phibes III and that's certainly true in a sense in that the premise and concept is almost identical in that Price plays a strange larger than life character who extracts a grisly revenge on a group of professional people with an elaborate and creative series of murders. Theatre of Blood does though give Price a lot more dialogue than Phibes and he is clearly having the time of his life reciting all of these Shakespeare monologues as the insufferably pompous Lionheart. This is a very witty and stylish film with quotable dialogue and death scenes that you'll never forget.

It's a clever idea to pattern the deaths around violent scenes from Shakespeare. So, for example, you get a critic drowned in wine like the Duke of Clarence in Richard III and Michael Hordern ("We'll have no trouble here!") is hacked to death like Julius Caesar. The Titus Andronicus inspired death of Robert Morely is probably the most famous in this film although the Cymbeline influenced demise of Arthur Lowe in his bed is the one that scarred the childhood version of me the most when I first watched this film!

Theatre of Blood is witty and funny but it is a surprisingly nasty film at times - much nastier than the Phibes films. Does it go too far at times? Possibly. I personally find that Theatre of Blood does occasionally cross the line from being witty and funny and macabre into being a bit too grim and unpleasant. Maybe that's just me though because this film is a much loved cult classic and was the personal favourite of Vincent Price out of all the films he made. I slightly prefer the Phibes films (which seems to be an eccentric opinion because most people seem to find Theatre of Blood vastly superior) but Theatre of Blood is certainly a great film at its best.

One thing I love about Theatre of Blood is that it supplies what is essentially a leading man role for Ian Hendry. Hendry was a great actor but his career was somewhat blighted by his drinking so it's great to see him enjoying a really big part in Theatre of Blood. Diana Rigg is clearly enjoying herself too as Lionheart's daughter - although some of the disguises Edwina and Lionheart adopt in the film would surely not fool anyone! The derelict theatre which Lionheart uses as a base in the film is the Putney Hippodrome - which had been vacant for several years at the time.

I always find the gang of down and outs that serve as Lionheart's audience and henchmen in the film to be creepy. They must be cheaper than conventional criminal henchmen because they only require a few bottles of meths as payment! Theatre of Blood, though very camp and tongue in cheek, is a very stylish film with a nice score by Michael J. Lewis. Despite all the humour it's a scary film too and most definitely a full blooded horror. You genuinely feel a sense of unease and tension whenever one of the critics finds themselves trapped in the deadly web spun by Lionheart. More than anything though, Theatre of Blood is wonderful vehicle for Vincent Price and he gives arguably the most famous performance of his career - clearly relishing the role of nutty old Edward Lionheart.

THREADS (1984)

A BAFTA award winning television film written by Barry Hines and directed by Mick Jackson, Threads is a knockabout musical comedy which takes a whimsical look at war and nuclear paranoia. I'm only joking. Threads is the bleakest thing ever transmitted on British television. It is beyond harrowing. The most terrifying thing about Threads is that this isn't science fiction or horror fantasy. It depicts something that - God forbid - could actually happen. Threads depicts a nuclear strike on Britain through the prism of ordinary people in the city of Sheffield. Most of the country is wiped out, millions die, there is blindness and radiation sickness, society collapses, and the survivors find themselves living in a grim new Stone Age. Threads is terrifying and sobering - as it should be. This is a very real seeming, ground level look at the consequences of the unthinkable happening.

Threads was made at a time when Cold War tensions were

very much a part of the news. It's little wonder that it greatly affected those who saw it. Not only was Threads harrowing but it depicted an event that could conceivably happen. Like The War Game (which we'll discuss later), Threads makes a mockery of government 'how to survive' materials of the era. The government would be woefully unprepared for what would really happen and those who did somehow survive would find themselves in something akin to hell on earth. They actually show the preposterous Protect and Survive * film being broadcast in Threads.

The first part of Threads is a conventional kitchen sink drama where young couple Ruth (Karen Meagher) and Jimmy (Reece Dinsdale) learn they have a baby on the way and make plans to get married. We meet their families and get a window into their ordinary working-class lives. This is actually an important part of Threads because it underscores the main message of the drama. The message is that it is ordinary people who would suffer in the unthinkable event of a nuclear war. The people who started the war and made the decision to send the missiles flying would all be safely in secret underground bunkers. It would be you and me who would get incinerated or suffer radiation sickness - not the war mongering lunatics who were responsible for all of this madness in the first place.

So we meet all of these people and get an insight into their lives - and then we see those lives ended or turned into a living nightmare all in the blink of an eye. The film depicts a Soviet incursion into Iran as a catalyst for a showdown between the Soviet Union and the United States. It begins as a conventional war and then turns nuclear. As we follow the characters we see and hear news bulletins which suggest the crisis is getting more and more serious. This is all very ominous indeed. When the characters go out to stock up on supplies they find the shelves nearly empty and the prices ludicrously inflated. Having lived through the pandemic and cost of living crisis we know exactly how that feels today!

The cast are all fine in this and it probably helps that there are no big stars or faces that are too familiar because that might have been distracting. The most recognisable person here is Reece Dinsdale - who the following year starred in the sitcom Home to Roost with John Thaw. I always remember Dinsdale for the football hooligan drama ID. You might recognise too Rita Ray (who plays the mother of Dinsdale's character) too. Rita May played the mother of the pub landlord Ken in the enjoyable but short lived BBC sitcom Early Doors.

Threads was meticulously researched and contains a lot of chilling factual information about what would actually happen not only in the immediate aftermath of a nuclear bomb dropping but also in the years and decades which followed. Not just radiation sickness (if you even survived the blast that is) but nuclear winter and freezing cold, shortage of food and water, ultraviolet light which would render many people blind, no hospitals, a collapse of law and order (which means murder and rape would be commonplace), disease, and general misery and squalor.

One of the most chilling aspects to the film is where we see Sheffield city council trying to organise things in a basement after the blast. They have emergency powers and talk about how they should not give food to those in heavy radiation areas because those people are already dead. They also talk about how they also need to hoard some food as a motivation to make people work. These council folk are soon all dead anyway. The blast was much bigger than they expected and they find themselves trapped by rubble until they suffocate. The council bigwigs are a microcosm of authority as a whole. One of the most frightening things about Threads is that the authorities would clearly not be able to cope with a nuclear ravaged country. There would be little they could do.

In the film we see gas masked soldiers guarding food supplies and shooting looters and protesters. The population of Britain is reduced to about four million - medieval levels. The survivors are disease ravaged and dressed in rags. They have to eat rats and all around is rubble and destruction. Crops don't grow anymore and technology is destroyed. There are many unforgettable scenes in the film. The children watching a tape of Words and Pictures (a kids TV show) in the ruined classroom. By the end of the film the children are speaking a primitive broken form of English - even language has been lost in the apocalypse. People are being shot over a husk of bread.

The sequence where the nuclear attack happens is probably the most terrifying thing ever broadcast on British television. The warning siren sounds and people, still out shopping and going about their business, are doomed. A woman wets herself in the street, Woolworths explodes, people burn, a mushroom cloud dominates the sky. It is the worst nightmare you can imagine. There is no relief in Threads whatsoever. No hope or indication that things might get better. The film becomes more and more grim as it goes on. Threads has a chilling final coda but all of it is chilling and it remains one of the most unsettling things ever broadcast on television. Threads is probably not something you'll be in a rush to view again but it is an important film that everyone should watch. If this film doesn't make you want to stick a CND badge on the wall then nothing will.

* Protect and Survive was a public information series produced by the British government during the late 1970s and early 1980s. The purpose of Protect and Survive was to advise the population on what to do in the event of a nuclear strike on the United Kingdom. There were leaflets prepared and a series of twenty short television films animated by Richard Taylor Cartoons. This was all highly classified and - thankfully - Protect and Survive was never broadcast. If the bomb had dropped though, or nuclear armageddon was deemed imminent, then the animated Protect and Survive series would have jammed every television channel. It would likely have been the last thing that millions of people ever watched.

Years later, with the Cold War thawed somewhat and nuclear war (hopefully) less of a realistic proposition, Protect and

Survive was released as something of a Cold War/nuclear paranoia historical artifact. You can even watch it on YouTube these days. And what a truly creepy artefact it is. Protect and Survive is narrated by Patrick Allen, a former actor who used his rich theatrical voice to carve out a later career as a voiceover artist and continuity announcer. Somehow, it's the absolute mundanity of Protect and Survive that makes it terrifying. Allen coldly and briskly narrates as if he's commenting on a plumbing manual. Each new chapter is heralded by a jaunty electronic beep that is strangely harrowing given the subject matter and there is probably no more frightening moment in the series than when they play the warning siren which will signal that the country is under nuclear attack.

The actual advice in the films seems preposterously useless. It is the sort of stuff that Raymond Briggs spoofed in his classic graphic novel When the Wind Blows. The population are advised to stay at ground level (great news for people living in high rise blocks) and told that cupboards under the stairs are good places to take shelter. You are advised to close your curtains - as if this is going to make any difference whatsoever when Soviet warheads start detonating! Protect and Survive states that two days must pass after the detonation before it is safe to venture outside again. Two days? That sounds ludicrously optimistic.

There are further bizarre passages like this in Protect and Survive - "If there is no solid cover, lie flat in a ditch or a hole, and cover your head face and your hands as fast as you can with some of your clothes. If you hear the fallout warning, seek the nearest and best cover as quickly as you can. But before entering the building or cover, brush or shake off any fallout dust you may have picked up and get rid of it. Change your outer clothing if you can. Stay under cover." So, if you happen to be outside when the bomb drops, just lay in a ditch and make sure to brush that pesky radiated dust off afterwards!

The animator Richard Taylor had this to say about the films -

"A lot of this advice was well intentioned but foolish. I don't know if people really thought lying in a ditch would give any protection from a nuclear bomb. But I thought that if there was going to be any kind of nuclear war, it was obviously better to have some sort of official advice than nothing at all." So perhaps this was the real purpose of Protect and Survive. They knew the information was largely pointless. It was there to offer a small crumb of comfort to anyone who had survived and give them the impression that the 'powers that be' were still functioning in some form or other. One would hardly say the films were reassuring though.

There is something deeply weird and disturbing about Protect and Survive with the electronic sound effects, chintzy animation, and velvet throated narration by Patrick Allen talking about where to store dead bodies as you drink water from a toilet cistern. Yes, civilisation as we know it may be ending but at least you have Patrick Allen to advise you on where you might best store tins of canned soup. Thank heavens they never had to broadcast this for real.

TRIANGLE (2009)

Triangle is a 2009 psychological horror thriller film written and directed by Christopher Smith. This film is a British/Australian co-production. Smith put himself on the map with Creep and Severance and Triangle is arguably his best film. This is a horror film with a time loop premise. The same thing being repeated. This device is not exactly original but it works well in Triangle and the film is much better than you probably expect it to be.

The film stars Melissa George as Jess, a woman with an autistic son who goes on a boating trip with some friends. When the boat sinks they end up taking refuge on an ocean liner that seems to have been abandoned. But Jess has a powerful sense of deja vu. She feels as if she's been on this ship before...

Triangle is one of those films that you don't go out of your way to watch but if you do take the time you'll be glad that you didn't miss it. I think I probably first saw this film on the Horror channel and had no idea at the time that it was made by the same person who did Severance. Triangle is like a Twilight Zone episode and seems to be patterned after films like Groundhog Day. I like the way the film essentially loops back in on itself in the last act.

Jess is trapped in a repeating loop and if you are familiar with Greek mythology (the name of the ship is a clue) you'll probably realise what is going on. "Aeolus. Aeolus was the Greek god of the winds and the father of Sisyphus, the man condemned by the gods to the task of pushing a rock up a mountain only to have it roll back down again."

The abandoned liner makes a good location and credit to the production for using a real liner and not resorting to CGI and green screens. The group start to die on the liner and Jess realises that she might be behind it all. She encounters future or even past versions of herself. Can she break out of the loop or is her fate sealed?

The film is inventive and moves at a breakneck speed once it gets going. Melissa George continues her mid career divergence into horror and really throws herself into the part, making a convincingly desperate and tough main character. The fight scenes are well staged the director keeps his camera moving as we follow Jess around the ship. The little payoffs, as Jess realises that she has been through these scenarios before, are both spine tingling and strangely moving.

This film is very much the Melissa George show and the other cast members don't really register much. That's fine though because Melissa George is up to the task of carrying the film on her shoulders. Triangle is not exactly a lavish film but it is well made on the budget they had the liner makes a good spooky location for the bulk of the story. The conclusion of the film is quite moving and will leave you thinking it afterwards. Maybe the story doesn't completely stand up to forensic scrutiny but it's a very inventive twist on something that has been done before in different genres. This horror tinged take on the recurring time loop is compelling and well played by the cast. It's a film that deserved a wider audience. Triangle is not what you would describe as a classic but it does what it sets out to do very well and is certainly worth watching.

28 DAYS LATER (2002)

28 Days Later is considered to a classic horror film by many and it is very British so I decided to include it in the book. I should point out though that it isn't my favourite thing. I'm not as big a fan of this film as many others - and that's fine because we all have different opinions. 28 Days Later was directed by Danny Boyle and written by Alex Garland. The film is a British riff on George A Romero's 'Dead' series of zombie films and also borrows rather liberally from John Wyndham's Day of the Triffids novel. 28 Days Later begins in a medical research unit where chimpanzees are being used to experiment with a contagious virus known as 'RAGE'.

However, things go very badly wrong when animal rights protesters break into the lab and free the animals. Twenty-eight days later, Jim (Cillian Murphy) wakes up in a deserted hospital and wanders outside to find an equally deserted London with overturned buses and litter on the breeze. After being attacked by a rabid, crazed priest, Jim realises something very strange has happened to the population but is rescued by survivors Mark (Noah Huntley) and Selena (Naomie Harris). They find other survivors in the form of cabbie Frank (Brendan Gleeson) and his teenage daughter Hannah (Megan Burns) and resolve to head for Manchester where a military signal is broadcasting a message of hope...

Shot mostly on digital video on a very modest budget, 28 Days Later is well directed by the inventive Danny Boyle with some striking images and visceral moments. It contains barely a single original idea and fans of Romero's Dawn of the Dead and Day of the Dead in particular will have a strong sense of deja vu during many of the sequences that unfold here. The opening scenes of Jim wandering around a desolate London are nicely done (presumably shot at the crack of dawn or something) and develop a mildly eerie atmosphere that heightens the viewer's curiosity but, in addition to ripping off Day of the Triffids right down to the hospital opening, this sequence is obviously influenced by the masterful beginning to 1985's Day of the Dead where a small group of characters land a helicopter in a deserted Florida street of windblown newspapers.

One difference between this and the Romero series is that the 'zombies' here run instead of shuffling around which is both a plus and a minus. A sequence in an underpass where the 'infected' appear and frantically chase down a stationary car the characters are trying to start generates some nice tension but, on the whole, I find Romero's zombies creepier because they just shuffle around and occasionally trap (and eat!) someone who hasn't been paying enough attention to their surroundings. The scenes where characters are caught by the infected are also rather anti-climatic and never really scary enough. They just tend to shake a lot and sort of throw up over their victims.

The film is a bit vague about the virus, although I suppose Romero never really explained the explanation for the outbreak in his own films. "It started as rioting," says Selena. "But right from the beginning you knew this was different. Because it was happening in small villages, market towns. And then it wasn't on the TV any more. It was in the street outside. It was coming in through your windows. It was a virus. An infection. You didn't need a doctor to tell you that. It was the blood. It was something in the blood. By the time they tried to evacuate the cities it was already too late. Army blockades were overrun. And that's when the exodus started." The early adventures of our small group of survivors are reasonably interesting although the film is a tad mawkish dealing with the characters attempts to find family members at times.

The film is quite interesting for a period when it switches to a military compound containing a small group of soldiers led by Christopher Eccleston's creepy Major Henry West but almost collapses entirely when West's plans are revealed and Jim turns into Tarzan running around the woods at night to a thumping soundtrack. The depiction of the military types in the film is so predictable. There is one excellent sequence where the compound, which is essentially a sort of stately home, comes under attack at night and the soldiers blast the infected to smithereens. Loudmouth cockney soldier Corporal Mitchell (Ricci Harnett), who sadly turns into a tedious caricature of a character, does initially have a few funny lines. I did laugh I must admit when he shouted "What do you want, a sweetie? Keep firing you ****!" to a fellow soldier during the skirmish.

West has an infected specimen (Mailer) chained up outside to monitor and study which is quite creepy but clearly inspired by Dr Logan's pet zombie 'Bub' in Day of the Dead. I must say I found that the ending to 28 Days Later didn't work. There is a far better and more effective alternate ending on the extras which they really should have used instead. One of the problems with the tiny budget is that occasionally, especially in suburbia, 28 Days Later does feel like you are watching an ITV drama or something rather than a feature film but, on the whole, I think Boyle did a good job.

One of the most chilling moments in 28 Days Later comes when West quietly tells one of his men to slow down. I won't reveal the context of the words for fear of spoilers but it's a nice piece of acting by Eccleston who is probably the most interesting presence here despite his 'posh' accent wavering on a few occasions a bit like Sean Bean's did as 006 in GoldenEye. I like a lot of 28 Days Later but the characters were not terribly memorable and I didn't care too much for the last act where everyone goes mad at the country mansion. Overall, I suspect my love of George A Romero clouded my view of 28 Days Later. It's an obvious criticism but 28 Days Later often comes across as a diluted shadow of George A Romero's back catalogue. Still, there IS some great stuff in 28 Days Later. It has plenty of atmosphere early on and some highly inventive direction.

TWINS OF EVIL (1971)

Twins of Evil was directed by John Hough. It is the third and final installment in Hammer Film Productions' Karnstein Trilogy, following The Vampire Lovers (1970) and Lust for a Vampire (1971). The film is set in 19th-century Europe and revolves around twin sisters, Maria (Mary Collinson) and Frieda (Madeleine Collinson), who move to a small village to live with their strict uncle Gustav Weil (Peter Cushing). Gustav is a religious nut and spends all of his spare time hunting alleged witches. That man definitely needs a new hobby if you ask me. Table tennis or something like that. Suffice to say, he isn't a barrel of laughs.

The sisters' arrival coincides with the rise of a local vampire cult led by Count Karnstein (Damien Thomas). Frieda falls under the spell of the count and becomes a vampire, while Maria tries to resist his influence. The twins' contrasting choices create a rift between them as they become entangled in a battle of good versus evil...

By the way, does the stirring intro theme to Twins of Evil sound familiar? It should do. The famous theme song (by Lolita Ritmanis) to the Justice League cartoon is clearly stolen from the opening title music to Twins of Evil. I'm surprised that Ritmanis actually got away with that brazen piece of musical theft. Twins of Evil gives you most of what you'd expect from a Hammer vampire caper and the clever idea to cast the cute Malta born twins Mary and Madeleine Collinson (who were both dubbed) gives the film an extra novelty and appeal.

Mary and Madeleine Collinson were Playboy Playmates of the month in October 1970 - which would explain how they got in the film. They said the reason they didn't have much of an acting career after 1971 is that they only wanted to work together and most films obviously don't have any need of twins as characters. The Collinson twins are surprisingly plausible as 19th-century ladies. It helps too that it is very difficult to tell them apart - which makes the fact that one of them turns evil more poignant.

Twins of Evil also supplies Peter Cushing with another chance to play an unsympathetic character and he more than makes the most of it. Gustav Weil is the sort of person who would happily burn his own granny if someone said she was a witch. Damien Thomas is a suave villain and there's a fairly sizeable heroic role for David Warbeck. Warbeck later became a cult actor for B-pictures and horror movies in Italy. Warbeck apparently tested to be James Bond several times too.

One of the strengths of Twins of Evil lies in its atmospheric visuals, which paint a vivid and haunting picture of the era. The Gothic architecture, decaying mansions, and dark forests perfectly complement the eerie storyline, creating a palpable sense of dread and unease. The cinematography highlights the film's attention to detail, allowing viewers to fully immerse themselves in this macabre world. Twins of Evil is probably not quite vintage Hammer but it is a lot of fun and worth watching for the Collinson twins alone.

VILLAGE OF THE DAMNED (1960)

Village of the Damned was directed by Wolf Rilla and based on the 1957 novel The Midwich Cuckoos by John Wyndham. The plot concerns the sleepy village of Midwich, where the entire population mysteriously falls unconscious for 24 hours. When they wake up, it transpires that every woman of child-bearing age is now pregnant. The children born from these pregnancies possess powerful telepathic abilities and display cold, emotionless behaviour.

The eerie and unsettling story follows the psychological and physical effects on the village and its inhabitants as they struggle to cope with the malevolent and manipulative children. As the children grow older, their telepathic powers become increasingly dangerous, causing panic among the villagers. A local professor and the village doctor work together to uncover the children's true nature and find a way to stop their destructive influence.

One of the strengths of Village of the Damned lies in its ability to create a palpable atmosphere of dread and unease from the very beginning. The film opens with a striking sequence when every living thing within a certain radius suddenly loses consciousness for several hours. This gripping event sets the tone for the rest of the film, leaving the audience on edge, wondering what could possibly occur next. The film's black and white cinematography, crafted by Geoff Mulligan, adds to the overall sense of foreboding and effectively accentuates the starkness of the small English village setting. The use of tight angles and close-ups enhances the feeling of confinement and intensifies the suspense as the disturbing events unfold.

George Sanders delivers an excellent portrayal of Gordon Zellaby, a rational and inquisitive scientist who becomes a central figure in attempting to understand and control the extraordinary children. Sanders successfully conveys a mix of concern, curiosity, and an underlying sense of fear as he confronts the unknown. Barbara Shelley's performance as Anthea Zellaby, Gordon's wife, is equally commendable, capturing the genuine distress and compassion of a mother facing an increasingly dire threat to her family.

While Village of the Damned is generally paced well with a steady build-up of tension, it occasionally suffers from slow moments in its second act, where the story relies heavily on the scientific investigation of the unusual children. Although these sections are necessary to convey the theme of human curiosity and the desire for understanding, they may feel less engaging to some viewers.

One of the most memorable aspects of this film is the portrayal of the children. Played by a group of unknown child actors, these young performers bring an uncanny quality to their roles, emphasising the children's otherworldly nature. Their collectively stoic and emotionless expressions coupled with their strange telepathic abilities create an eerie and unsettling atmosphere throughout the film, augmenting the suspense and horror. The narrative of Village of the Damned offers a thought-provoking exploration of human nature in the face of unknown and potentially dangerous forces. It delves into the ethical dilemmas involved in dealing with extraordinary and possibly malevolent children. The film questions notions of empathy and morality while delving into the frightening implications of power wielded by those without moral guidance.

In 1964, there was a sort of unofficial sequel with Children of the Damned. This film got a mixed reception but it is worth watching - not least because it supplies Ian Hendry with a leading role. Children of the Damned has a different concept in that it is about super powered children (who are not identical) in different parts of the world. Village of the Damned was later remade by John Carpenter in 1995 with the story transplanted (in fairly faithful fashion) to California. Carpenter's remake is fairly forgettable - although it is nice to see Christopher Reeve in one of his last roles before his awful riding accident. The remake of Village of the Damned is competently made but just not terribly exciting and a film unlikely to win John Carpenter any new fans.

THE WAR GAME (1965)

"On almost the entire subject of nuclear weapons, on the problems of their possession, on the effects of their use, there is now practically a total silence in the press, in official publications, and on television. There is hope in any unresolved and unpredictable situation. But is there a real hope to be found in the silence? The world's stockpile of nuclear weapons has doubled in the last 5 years, and now is the equivalent to almost 20 tons of high explosives to every man, woman, and child on the planet. This stockpile is still steadily growing."

The War Game is a sobering docu-drama about the effects of a nuclear strike on Britain. The focus is on towns in Kent struggling to cope with all the death and destruction and those injured. The War Game was directed by Pete Watkins and deemed so shocking by the BBC that they decided not to screen it. It won a documentary Oscar but was not screened on television until the 1980s. The film (which is only 50 or so minutes long) is a mock documentary and all the more chilling for the impassive matter of fact way it approaches the subject (with narration by Peter Graham and Michael Aspel).

After the build up to war, with evacuations from London, the bombs drop and The War Game presents a picture of hell on earth as bodies pile up, people are blinded, suffer radioactive burns, the authorities shoot looters, and so on. Watkins pulls no punches in showing us what would happen to people if the bomb had dropped during the Cold War. The film is not only a harrowing piece of television but a critique of futile, laughable, and misleading 'how to survive' government propaganda.

The War Game was clearly the biggest influence on the 1984 film Threads. Both share similar sequences of the police shooting looters, burned people, and bodies piled up. What is the difference between The War Game and Threads? I suppose the key difference is that The War Game is made in the style of a fly on the wall documentary whereas Threads is a television drama. Threads was able to go slightly further than The War Game when it comes to death and the grim reality of nuclear conflict but The War Game is no picnic that's for sure. Children are blinded, we see carts full of dead people with burned faces, and the sequence where firemen are thrown around by a firestorm is utterly terrifying.

There is a lot of (highly alarming) factual information in The War Game. The narrator tells us that Britain, due to its Vulcan bomber fleet and air bases, has more Soviet military targets than any country in Europe. The narrator also tells us that because Soviet nuclear warheads are vulnerable to being destroyed on the ground, in the event of nuclear war they'd probably just launch all of them to completely wipe out their enemies. That's all bad news for 1960s Blighty. We'd be blown to smithereens.

The War Game says at one point that the chances of this all happening for real by 1980 are very high. Thankfully that didn't transpire. Much like Threads, a big part of The War Game is how civilisation and law and order would collapse in this nightmare scenario. We see the police who ration the food killed by looters. The War Game tells us that the police would have the task of shooting the badly injured and sick in order to 'put them out of their misery'. The army would have the task of burning bodies because there would be too many to bury.

When this film was made, World War 2 was obviously a much more recent event. So you get a number of comparisons to that conflict. A nuclear attack on Britain, we learn, would be like the bombing of Dresden on a much bigger scale - only worse. A lot worse. The War Game was filmed in Kent and used local actors. The acting is pretty good on the whole and the fly on the wall style of the film makes it feel a bit like an early found footage film at times. The narrator tells us that Kent was 'lightly' hit. If this carnage and destruction is 'light' then heaven only knows what the worst affected areas are like. That's one of the most chilling things about The War Game. It presents hell on Earth and tells us this is the best case scenario!

The background to conflict in The War Zone is China invading South Vietnam and the United States intervening. This leads to the Soviets declaring they will invade West Berlin if the Americans do not withdraw from Vietnam. It is the Americans who initiate the nuclear conflict by launching their missiles first. There are some interesting moral questions posed in the film - like what would be the point of nuclear retaliation against a country that had nuked you? You would be killing millions of civilians and children out of revenge. Would this be justified or simply pointless?

Some detected an anti-religious sentiment in the film because there are a number of church ministers seeming to justify nuclear weapons and war. These though were real comments from church people so I don't think anyone should get too up in arms - and they were an exception rather than the rule. I'm fairly sure that the vast majority of the clergy were opposed to war and nuclear destruction! The film ends by tell us that nuclear stockpiles are rising all the time and asks why there is not more coverage of this fact in the media. The War Game is plainly the biggest influence on Threads and a remarkable piece of television. Grim nuclear war dramas were all the rage in the eighties but The War Game is as chilling as any of them and got there a few decades before The Day After and Threads.

WHEN THE WIND BLOWS (1986)

Yet more nuclear paranoia next I'm afraid. When the Wind Blows was first published in 1982 and is a graphic novel by the great illustrator and author Raymond Briggs. The book is about a nuclear attack on Britain by the Soviet Union seen entirely from the perspective of Jim and Hilda Bloggs, an old-fashioned retired couple living a peaceful and happy existence in a remote cottage in the countryside. Briggs was best known at the time for wonderful children's books like Father Christmas and (my own cult favourite) Fungus The Bogeyman. When The Wind Blows, a bleak, angry, political story, saw the author produce his first adult work and a book which many regard to be his finest hour. The 1986 animated film version was directed by Jimmy Murakami and features the voices of John Mills and Peggy Ashcroft as the two main characters.

When The Wind Blows begins with Jim Bloggs frequently reading the newspapers in the library to keep up to date with the 'international situation' although we quickly discover that neither Jim or Hilda are the most up to date or sophisticated people in the world. They both see any crisis in the rosy glow of their World War 2 memories and if everyone pulled together and survived that one then there is nothing to fear from a new war. Or so they think. As they have their dinner there is a sudden radio broadcast from the Prime Minister. The threat of an imminent nuclear attack is not quite grasped by Hilda- who promptly attends to the pudding and later suggests to Jim that he should wear his old clothes for the bomb and his new ones afterwards.

Jim meanwhile is slightly more prepared although he calls computers 'commuters' and assumes that Field Marshall Montgomery is still in charge of the army. Jim has a leaflet from the library called 'The Householders Guide To Survival'. He's soon following it to the letter and unscrewing doors to make an indoor shelter despite Hilda's annoyance at the mess he is making. The leaflet that Jim has is, of course, a complete waste of time but he follows it with enthusiasm, confident that, just like World war 2, they'll all pull together and emerge on VE Day. Because we won the war all those years ago, Jim naturally assumes that the 'Powers that be' always know what is best.

A big part of the effect of When The Wind Blows comes from placing such a dark story within the confines of cosy and comforting characters. Jim and Hilda are a deliberately normal and down to earth old couple. They could be your grandparents and that's the most powerful thing about the story. It gives them character, humour, memories, flashbacks and an ordinary down to earth run of the mill quality that most will relate to.

Briggs did not shy away from the ramifications of a nuclear attack - radiation sickness for example - and his anger is palpable. Those responsible for a nuclear attack will follow it all from a bunker. The innocent, the Jim and Hilda's of this world, will be wiped out. By filling the story with Jim and Hilda's nostalgic memories of World War 2, Briggs powerfully expresses his anger that so many memories and lives could be wiped out merely by someone pressing a button somewhere. The film manages to capture this sense of outrage.

There are some terrifying images in the film of weapons of mass destruction like a lone missile on a lonely plain. The nuclear blast is a chilling flash of white. The government leaflets of the era are given a good kicking. Nonsense like sleeping under a door or getting inside a potato sack. Jim phones up his son and asks a question about the angle of the shelter he wants to build and is met with a response of slightly hysterical laughter. This is the view of Briggs of course. If the country was about to be hit by a nuclear strike and you were in the firing line what would be the point of getting in a potato sack or painting your windows!

It goes without saying that When The Wind Blows is ultimately a bleak film. It was made during a time when nuclear armageddon seemed like a real threat and to watch it is to be taken back to an era of chilling paranoia and fear amped up by the cold war between the West and the now defunct Soviet Union. Throughout the story Jim Bloggs mixes up the 'Russkies' with the 'Jerrys'. The idea that our World War 2 'allies' Russia are now the big threat simply serves to confuse Jim. Jim and Hilda's fogged memories somehow see Stalin as a loveable Uncle.

Jim has a naive belief in the 'Powers that be' but we know that no one is going to help them. The 'Powers that be' are the ones to fear in When The Wind Blows. Like other anti-bomb creations of the time - the television drama Threads - When The Wind Blows is a powerful plea against a war that will have unthinkable consequences. When The Wind Blows is both an original approach to the subject and a devastating black comedy. When the two characters enter a very real nuclear nightmare, When the Wind Blows becomes as disturbing as any live action horror film. This is a heartbreaking and compelling film.

THE WICKER MAN (1973)

As far as British horror films go, none are more cultish and revered as The Wicker Man. The film is inspired by the David Pinner novel Ritual and is now regarded to be a classic. However, this wasn't always the case. The distributor initially refused to release The Wicker Man, even in Britain. The theatrical version was then cut down to 88 minutes with Christopher Lee calling it a 'shadow' of the film they'd made. Legend has it that the original negative of the full length version was used as landfill in the M3 motorway in England! Although restored in DVD editions in later decades, the full uncut version of the film has yet to emerge from whatever dusty vault it might be hiding.

The film's musical arranger, Gary Carpenter said: "I have a vivid memory of having to score a phenomenally complex dream sequence for Howie, which was like post-scoring an animation, it was so intricate. The fades and dissolves and extensive use of library footage for this sequence seriously dented the budget. Despite Robin Hardy's enthusiasm for it and its inclusion in what I assumed at the time to be 'The Director's Cut', I have never seen reference made to it again and it is in no existing version of the film." It's a shame that The Wicker Man was treated so shoddily on its initial release but the enduring legend and popularity of the film has at least given it a happy ending.

The story has Edward Woodwood as a repressed policeman named Sgt Howie sent to a remote Scottish island from the mainland to investigate a child's disappearance. He soon realises that everyone there is under the spell of the spooky island leader Lord Summerisle (Christopher Lee). Howie, a devout Christian, is shocked that the locals have turned to paganism and treat both his authority and his beliefs with a mocking indifference. He begins to suspect that the missing child might be earmarked for a sacrificial fertility ritual but the case proves to be more troubling than he'd ever suspected.

The Wicker Man is beautifully paced and reveals its secrets in a clever and often strange way with a genuinely authentic sense of location and atmosphere. The film was shot in Gatehouse of Fleet, Newton Stewart, Kirkcudbright and a few scenes in the village of Creetown in Dumfries and Galloway, as well as Plockton in Ross-shire. Britt Ekland had to apologise after calling Galloway the bleakest place on earth. Ekland doesn't seem to look back on the film fondly. "It was not an enjoyable experience at all. We shot it in south-west Scotland on a massive cliff with the sea pounding away below. Filming started in mid or late October and went on for about six weeks. It was very windy and cold but the film was supposed to be set in summer so we were not allowed any overcoats."

The film was shot near winter and fake plastic blossoms had to be put on the trees. The aerial photography was partly done in South Africa because Scotland in October had bare trees. The film is well directed by Robin Hardy and the script by Anthony Shaffer is clever and ambitious. Shaffer and Hardy became estranged after making The Wicker Man and Shaffer later said that Hardy was a terrible director - although this seems rather harsh given the quality of the film. Shaffer apparently felt that Edward Woodward and Britt Eklund were miscast. Scottish jazz singer Annie Ross dubbed Ekland's voice and Ekland only found out much later. "I knew my singing was not so fabulous but I thought my Scottish accent was pretty good. Again, nobody told me so there wasn't much I could say about it." Peter Cushing and Michael York were offered the role of Sgt Howie but both were unavailable.

Despite Shaffer's concerns, it's hard to think of Woodward's passionate and vulnerable performance as anything but an asset to the film. Woodward was pleased to be offered something that was not like the Callan role he was associated with at the time and he responds with a terrific performance in The Wicker Man. This might well too be Christopher Lee's finest hour in terms of acting. His Lord Summerisle is incredibly suave and patronising to Woodward's Howie, amused at the policeman's inability to grasp what is really happening and doubly amused at him for being an uptight Christian. "I think I could turn and live with animals. They are so placid and self-contained. They do not lie awake in the dark and weep for their sins. They do not make me sick discussing their duty to God. Not one of them kneels to another or to his own kind that lived thousands of years ago. Not one of them is respectable or unhappy, all over the earth."

This was Christopher Lee's favourite film out of the many he made and he saw The Wicker Man as a way to break out of his Dracula typecasting. Lee was furious that the film wasn't marketed very well and urged journalists to watch it. He found the subject matter of the film fascinating. "As a young man I was always fascinated by the occult," said Lee. "I'd read Frazer's The Golden Bough, a great deal of which is about Celtic belief, sacrifice, superstition, and so on. So I was already very well versed in the subject matter."

A horror film with a great understanding of atmosphere, The Wicker Man has a real sense of local colour and location, weirdness, and a twist ending which is quite shocking when you first watch the film. The folk music and pagan rituals that serve as a backdrop are at once both charming and foreboding - the line veering towards the downright creepy when characters resort to their costumes for the big festival at the end. The Wicker Man is a haunting and absorbing film that repays a few repeat viewings. There is nothing else quite like it.

By the way, many years later there was a sequel to The Wicker Man - though it is a film few have seen. The Wicker Tree is a 2011 sequel to 1973's The Wicker Man - both directed by Robin Hardy. The Wicker Man is regarded to be one of the greatest British horror films ever made. This wretched sequel is an amateurish waste of everyone's time. Hardy based The Wicker Tree on his novel Cowboys for Christ. The ludicrous story has two young American Christians named Steve (Henry Garrett) and Beth Boothby (Britannia Nicol) sent to 'heathen' Scotland to teach them about God. They end up being invited to a village by Sir Lachlan Morrison (Graham McTavish) and, well, if you've seen the original film, you'll have a good idea of what eventually happens.

Nothing in this terrible film makes much sense and it's little wonder that it didn't find a theatrical release. The notion that Scotland is some primitive backwater is preposterous for a film made in 2011. You'd think Hardy would know better. The two American leads can't act to save their lives and the film plays like cheap student film shot with a camcorder. Most of the actors here seem embarrassed and aware that they've ended up in a real stinker. Foyle's War actor Honeysuckle Weeks is also in the film and frequently required to take her clothes off.

Christopher Lee was going to be the lead of the film but had to pull out because of illness. Lucky for him really. He has a cameo instead with the lead villain role going to Graham McTavish. What this film illustrates perfectly is how the original Wicker Man was lightning in a bottle. You just can't replicate the wonderfully strange and chilling nature of that 'folk horror' film. Robin Hardy (who hardly made any films in between these two Wicker Man pictures) should really have left The Wicker Man to stand alone as an undoubted classic of British cinema. If you do love the original it is best to pretend that The Wicker Tree doesn't exist.

WHISTLE AND I'LL COME TO YOU (1968)

Whistle and I'll Come to You is a classic BBC adaption of an MR James ghost story. It was produced for the BBC's Omnibus arts programme in 1968 and directed by Jonathan Miller. In Whistle and I'll Come to You, which is 42 minutes long in total, Michael Horden plays the crumpled Professor Parkins, an eccentric and solitary academic who arrives at a small seaside hotel in Norfolk for a walking and reading holiday.

On one of his frequent brisk and breezy walks along the chilly, deserted coastline, Parkins discovers an old cemetery that is slowly sinking over a cliff and notices an object that appears to be a whistle of some sort made out of bone. "Finders keepers," mutters Parkins and promptly places it in his pocket to take home. When he cleans the whistle out later in his room with a penknife, the Professor notices a strange inscription which, once translated into Latin, seems to give a vaguely supernatural warning (Who is this who is coming?). Parkins blows on the whistle and thinks nothing more of it - until that is he starts to be plagued by chilling nightmares and finds his secure and logical outlook on life increasingly challenged in a terrifying manner...

A cult favourite, Whistle and I'll Come to You usually seems to make an appearance on those 'scariest moment' compilation shows and documentaries about spooky British television produced down the years and is generally thought of in fond terms. I've never read the story on which this is based but apparently the literary source featured a much younger and more precise Parkins rather than the wonderful Michael Hordern's enjoyably twitchy and slightly dotty character here.

In the book Parkins was on a golfing holiday but Hordern's character comments that he never plays the game and spends his holiday reading, walking on the beach over the sand dunes in gusty winds and, most of all, eating voraciously throughout much of the film.

The sight of Michael Hordern demolishing a grapefruit with relish as he discusses - with that great voice - philosophy and the supernatural with another guest at breakfast ("Delicious breakfast!" he murmurs to himself having moved onto the kipper) is always oddly compelling and rather good fun. Whether it's an apple and sandwich on the beach or a piece of toast in the hotel, Hordern brilliantly eats everything as if completely famished. Although shortish, the film is admirably unhurried and develops slowly at its own pace as Parkins settles into the sedate guest house.

Hordern's presence is a great boost to Whistle and I'll Come to You as Parkins wanders awkwardly through the story muttering to himself in a slightly befuddled manner, clearly uncomfortable with other people. There is a powerful sense of solitude and loneliness to Parkins, illustrated when the elderly proprietor (George Woodbridge) takes his bags up to his room at the beginning of the film and Hordern walks behind him, uncomfortably, with his hands behind his back, unsure of what to say.

Woodbridge, in a minor comic cameo, then mutters something that is completely incomprehensible but Parkins is uninterested in seeking clarity and (we sense) wants to be alone instead. Parkins only really springs to life and talks expansively when at breakfast where he finds himself ruminating on existential matters with The Colonel (Ambrose Coghill). These scenes are very absorbing as Hordern, continually eating his breakfast, excitedly blabbers away though avoiding eye-contact with his fellow guest - who he deliberately sits far away from.

"There are more things in philosophy than are dreamt of in heaven," says Parkins (after the other guest states the exact opposite) and is then unable to help himself from chuckling in a very satisfied manner at his own riposte. Although there is a bumbling quality to Hordern's character and we see he is a loner awkward with even the smallest human interaction, this is possibly a brilliant mind, if a rather self-satisfied one.

Miller is somewhat ambiguous in his handling of the material and the increasingly scary and strange happenings that atmospherically swirl around Parkins. It could be either supernatural or all in a mind that is starting to fray around the edges - perhaps from loneliness. Ultimately the audience has to decide for themselves. Perhaps the most salient element to any good ghost or horror story is of course atmosphere and Whistle and I'll Come to You understands this concept beautifully.

The film has an incredibly rich and eerie air of dread, aided by the black and white photography, with the small hotel and its mostly empty rooms and numerous sequences of Horden walking the abandoned winter beaches, rubbing his hands together and shivering slightly as the wind whips around him. The bleak but interesting landscape makes for a wonderful backdrop as Parkins trudges about the sand-dunes, the sound-effects highlighting the almost ghostly moans and crashes of the sea breeze.

Everything is seen tightly through Parkins and, thankfully, Michael Hordern really holds everything together. Even if nothing is happening you find yourself absorbed in his quiet world of reading, munching food and walking the beach alone. The film would even have worked as a small character study I think even without the ghostly capers although the apparent encroachment of these dark forces into such a serene and mundane setting gives Whistle and I'll Come to You a very unsettling quality in its best moments.

Miller was, I suspect, more interested in the breakfast philosophy discussions and atmosphere of the piece than ghosts although Whistle and I'll Come to You does have some very famous moments towards the end that have frequently been cited as some of the most spine-tingling in British television history. While the film is not quite as scary as legend suggests, there are undoubtedly a couple of highly creepy moments that will certainly give anyone who hasn't seen them before a mild chill or two.

That these moments are isolated is a help and - although accomplished in a ridiculously homemade and inexpensive way - they are strangely effective with excellent use of mournful, slightly odd sound-effects, the film containing no music. The real chills here though also come from Hordern's bewildered reactions as Parkins begins helplessly muttering to himself, unwilling to accept that what he has seen is real but completely terrified nonetheless. I'll Come to You is very absorbing and quietly rewarding and the always very watchable Michael Hordern is superb as Parkins. A classic piece of spooky British television that is still well worth taking a look at today.

WITCHFINDER GENERAL (1968)

Witchfinder General (known in the US as Conqueror Worm) was directed by Michael Reeves. Reeves died at the age of 25 - which was a great tragedy for the British film industry. Who knows what he might have gone on to do. Witchfinder General was made on a modest budget but was a shocking film for its time. The film gives Vincent Price one of his most famous roles - that of Matthew Hopkins, a witchfinder during the English Civil War. The real witch trials were based on superstitious beliefs, religious hysteria, and confessions obtained through torture or duress. Believe it or not, if someone randomly accused you of being a witch then this was taken at face value and you would most likely end up being executed!

The character in this film was based on Matthew Hopkins (c. 1620-1647) - an English witchfinder who is known for his involvement in the witch trials that took place in East Anglia, England during the 17th century. He gained notoriety for his self-proclaimed expertise in identifying witches and played a significant role in the persecution and execution of numerous women accused of witchcraft. In those days superstition and belief in the occult allowed wicked and delusional people like Hopkins to flourish.

In the film, Hopkins and his assistant John Steame (Robert Russell) make enemies of a young Roundhead named Richard Marshall (Ian Ogilvy) when they mistreat his love Sarah (Hilary Dwyer). Witchfinder General is known for its graphic depiction of violence and torture, which was controversial at the time of its release. The film combines elements of horror, period drama, and psychological thriller, exploring themes of abuse of power, superstition, and morality.

One of the most striking aspects of Witchfinder General is its unflinching portrayal of violence and the insidious nature of abuse of power. The film boldly delves into the oppressive tactics and sadistic methods employed by Hopkins to extract confessions from supposed witches. I gather that Reeves wasn't too sure sure about the casting of Vincent Price in this film because he found Price a bit hammy in those AIP films. Price turns in a more serious performance in this film and he's terrific as this driven (driven in a completely deluded way of course) and heartless man.

Ian Ogilvy is also well cast as the dashing young Roundhead. Ogilvy was a Michael Reeves regular and later of course played Simon Templar in Return of the Saint. This film is quite harsh at times although the violence and torture seems tamer today than it must have done in 1968. It is commendable though the film approaches the subject in a fairly unflinching sort of way. Michael Reeves' direction, Vincent Price's memorable performance, and the captivating visuals all contribute to its powerful portrayal of a grim chapter in English history.

Milton Keynes UK
Ingram Content Group UK Ltd.
UKHW040751020224
437154UK00001B/98